The Five Phases of Successful Urban Leadership (K-8)

JACK HUNTER

THE FIVE PHASES OF SUCCESSFUL URBAN LEADERSHIP (K-8)

J. Hunter Venture Group

If you are interested in learning more about the services his company can provide, please contact him at contact@jhunterventuregroup.com.

Follow him on twitter at @chasestem or via his blog at www.jhunterventuregroup.com

Copyright © 2018 by Jack Hunter
Printed in the United States of America

ISBN 978-0-692-11686-9

JHVG Publishing

All rights reserved. This book or any portion thereof
may not be reproduced or used in any manner whatsoever
without the express written permission of the publisher
except for the use of brief quotations in a book review.

Cover design and text layout by Crysti Esper, Creative Edge, Monroe, Michigan

First Edition 10 9 8 7 6 5 4 3 2 1

DEDICATED TO

Max, Lilly, my wife Beth, and my mother Cherie,
for encouraging me to complete this important work.

Also, a special dedication to all the Urban Educators
in the world. Always remember you make a difference!

Table of Contents

Introduction

Chapter One: Learning Purpose 1

Chapter Two: Planning for Success 9

Chapter Three: Tinker 43

Chapter Four: Collaborate 61

Chapter Five: Integrate 71

Chapter Six: Fine Tune 89

Chapter Seven: Summary 135

Preface

HOW IT BEGAN

As a young man growing up in Cleveland, Ohio and experiencing urban education through my mother's career experiences, I had ambitions of taking on the world. I wanted to be the Michael Jordan of education. I chose the career of education with a focus on mathematics. This training would allow me to help in one of the areas students struggle with the most and also provide me with the career tools I needed to gain immediate employment. During my collegiate careers, my experiences further confirmed my desire to help urban children. With the excitement of being recently hired into a math specialist position, I finally had my opportunity. I quickly realized that a support position, where I only instructed classrooms once a week, would not yield the results I needed to fulfill my goal. The position limited my engagement with specific students and I needed my own classroom to make lasting change.

The Five Phases of Successful Urban Leadership (K-8)

I had the opportunity to move to Michigan and secure a position with Detroit Public Schools. I was hired to teach 7th and 8th-grade math and computers in a 100% free and reduced lunch school. This school was in a very high crime area and could have easily been the featured school in the hit movie "Lean on Me". It truly was a school in disarray and the students came to school for reasons other than to get an education. I finally had the opportunity I dreamed of! I now have the chance to motivate reluctant learners into self-motivated students.

Throughout the journey of reading this book, you will hear strategies I used in the classroom as well as how to turn a school around in a sensible, productive and moral way. This book will provide a granular approach to the change process.

With the current landscape of education, urban schools are not the anomaly anymore, they are the norm. This is why this book is so important for all educators. The American family has become more transient than ever and the principal, as the lead learner, must be empowered to continually learn how students with varying amounts of background knowledge are educated in the most demanding environments.

Change Lives Choose to Be an Urban Leader!

Introduction

A WELCOME TO AN ADVENTURE

> "THE SECRET TO SUCCESS IS TO FIND SOMETHING
> YOU LOVE TO DO SO MUCH, YOU CAN'T WAIT FOR THE SUN
> TO RISE TO DO IT OVER AGAIN"
>
> **CARMINE GALLO**

Welcome to your adventure as an Urban Leader. You committed to being a leader in an environment with high turnover and lack of continuity. There is hope! Throughout your journey as an Urban Leader and using this book as a guide, you will learn how to hone your leadership skills to maximize the effectiveness of your educators and how to motivate all your stakeholders to join in this crucial educational process. With steadfast vision and a willingness to put the organization before your career aspirations, change can occur in the most forgotten places. We are challenged with immense pressure as educators. We have increased accountability, high poverty, homelessness, an increase in students with disabilities, lack of credentialed educators and reduced funding. As a leader with skill and passion, you will learn how to move the consistent pieces around in your organization to assist the educators in reaching the same goal. The goal of all schools should be to improve the whole child. The whole child is more than a subjective grade on a report card. We must look for ways to engage our students in the learning process and continually challenge them to better themselves with the scaffolding support of an empathetic educator and instructional leader.

Throughout this book, I will give evidence of the items I have used successfully to create a school climate that is conducive to learning and growth. I will share with you the paradigm I developed to create the change process in my school. The same paradigm was used when I built my first business and eventually sold it to a large venture capital group. The framework, if followed, will keep you focused on the end goal which is student achievement and educating our children on the strategies of success. I will delve into multiple facets of school turn-around and bring the perspective of an entrepreneur and an educator into this book.

If you follow the ideas and framework of this book, you will be amazed at how your organization is re-created in the image of successful students. Growth and excitement are contagious. Therefore, when the leader models enthusiasm and works alongside the practitioners, the change will occur even more rapidly. I am both excited for you to apply these proven ideas and best practices into your learning establishment as well as anxious for the success that will occur as you delve into these research and evidence-based strategies.

1 LEARNING PURPOSE
TEACHING → PRINCIPAL

"You cannot discover new oceans unless you have the courage to lose sight of the shore"
Mac Anderson

The first day I walked into my Detroit Public Middle School classroom, I saw 37 students staring at me in my first period class. One student immediately asked me, "How long are you going to stay?" I asked the student why. He replied with a smirk, "Yeah. Teachers don't last here." They needed to know I cared and was invested in them before learning could occur. The leadership was absent; students were able to skip classes and come and go as they wanted. Students would use drugs in the school, fight, and have relationships in the visible common areas. No security was present, and this was the "norm" in this particular building. The students deserved more. How was I going to be able to get through to all students each period and make math exciting? I went home, regrouped and reached into my limited tool chest to set up a game plan.

I spent the first week watching and teaching with little or no participation and multiple levels of disruption. Therefore, my first task was to identify one commonality that I would have with the students. Basketball was the catalyst I was going to use to promote change. I began my next lesson telling a story about my young adult basketball career which included getting to play against players who eventually made it to the NBA. I brought in a Nerf basketball rim and hung it on the chalkboard. I immediately started to get their attention. The connection I needed was made! I used this catalyst and the statistics of the NBA to segway into math. Sure, statistics and probability were not the 1st standards in the "pacing guide," however; it was the hook that allowed me to introduce other topics. We would disseminate box scores from Detroit Pistons games and talk about percentages, probability, angles, and averages. When students participated in class, we would use the basketball hoop as a reward to emulate one of the players we were researching. This created a standard math language that we used in class. We would speak about players and their statistical averages. Another lesson entailed listening to a pre-recorded game, having the students record the statistics, then checking their work with the professional statisticians' report. This built confidence in some students who would tell me how much they used to hate math and didn't understand how it related to the real world. It wasn't just about math anymore, we were starting to communicate.

After I achieved my first obstacle, the second task was to make it evident that I would not lower my expectations. I expected every seventh and eighth grader to pass my class. Failure was not an option. This was easy to say, but oh so hard to execute. The previous year, zero students passed the Michigan Standardized Test in Math. I knew this was an almost impossible task to remedy in one year, but I was intent on giving it everything I had. I encouraged students, tutored and bribed them, walked to student's homes and talked to parents. I wanted to share my passion for math and offer parents support in learning essential Microsoft programs so they could assist their students with math homework. I made the computers in my classroom available for parents to use and assisted some parents with their resumes, if they wanted assistance. I never thought a 22-year-old could motivate adults older than myself to come and learn how to improve themselves. I had nine parents who came and took advantage of my computer offer. And I am pleased to say that four parents ended up getting jobs after I helped them with their resume. To me, I wanted to prove to myself that this could be scaled on a more significant basis. I did anything I could to get more face time with the students while I was instructing and securing parental support.

I fell short of my 100% goal of the students passing the state math assessment as only 52% passed. I felt like I let some of the students down, but I quickly realized I gave most of the students a zest for math, the confidence to persevere in school and to appreciate the need for math as a life skill. This year, to me, was a success. I did not have to remove any of the students from my classes and I refused to give up and give them the easy way out.

After the school year, we found out this Detroit Public School would be closing in the next year as the district was restructuring. I was afraid I would lose my job, as I had limited seniority in the system. Recently married and looking to start a family, I decided to venture into the business world through an entrepreneurial adventure. This would turn out to be a great life lesson, one in which molded me as the leader I am today. After six years in business, the path would see me build a successful multi-million-dollar company and furthermore, sell it to a Venture Capital Group. This journey of long hours provided me the position as a Regional Manager and finally, as the Chief Operating Officer. My experience in urban environments helped me welcome a diverse workforce which gave the company a step ahead of other competitors. The business was taking off and showing immense growth. However, while the business was highly profitable, having a young family, I felt something was missing from my life, purpose. Sure, I liked the money, tickets to sporting events and fancy dinners but I was not helping to change or impact anyone's life. I felt as if I were a robot with no purpose except to make money.

    I spent a lot of time with my family discussing a different career move. I thought back to what made me happy. After I quickly realized that it was not money, my mind shifted back to what my innate passion had always been, helping urban students!! I wanted to become a leader who would put true meaning in children's lives, to help the learners find their confidence and become a successful part of our community and society. I have the passion and leadership skills I needed and knew I was ready to make my passion my career. As Michael Fullan states, "Passion without talent is dangerous." Passion with skill, to me, is an unstoppable attribute that very few people can reach in their lifetime.

I started graduate school toward an administration degree and to follow my new goal. While I was in school obtaining my administration degree, I returned to teach mathematics in an urban classroom in the lowest performing school in Toledo, Ohio. I knew my family made a substantial financial sacrifice by my decision to serve others versus trying to maximize our own financial net worth. Nevertheless, my sound mind and body mattered more to my family. My wife and mother wanted me to be happy and eliminated any question or hesitation to my career change. With a previous weight off my shoulders, I began a new, yet very familiar journey. That school year, I was able to quickly turn the culture around in my classroom and my students outperformed everyone else with similar demographics. On the state assessment in mathematics the average student showed 2.75 years of growth in one year. The same tenacity I used in business to produce success was used to increase the aptitude of my students. But what was even more evident to my close circle of peers and mentors was that this is where I was supposed to be. I am a leader of people and I want to change other people's lives so they feel successful. I am a leader of educators committed to bettering the lives of their learners.

THE BEGINNING AS AN INSTRUCTIONAL LEADER

So, you are or aspire to be, a leader in your chosen educational field. Are you truly ready? When I was educated in the late 1980's and 1990's, students would come to classrooms and sit in straight rows and walk in straight lines. It was the norm, and that was the standard that was accepted by all stakeholders. The word *differentiation* was not in educational pedagogy or certainly not at the forefront. The classes I was educated in as a child were all either ability grouped or all taught with the same worksheet or chapter in the book. Most students were educated the same way. Educators grouped students based on levels and did not use flexible grouping, which is the norm in most productive schools today. Students with learning disabilities were often bussed to another school in the district and taught a curriculum that was far inferior to the mainstream curriculum. Imagine how many future electricians, plumbers or architects were not trained due to this mentality. This is the exact reason I wanted to write this book. **Every person, every child has a specific skill set that has value.** Our job as educators is to cultivate each student's abilities. This cannot be done with archaic ways of instruction. Contrary to what everyone reads and hears, it is not the teachers' fault. Principals must be leaders and model the kind of instructional pedagogy that is needed for students to prosper.

THE EDUCATIONAL HIRING PROCESS

When I was hired on Aug 1st as a principal, I was given three weeks to open the school for students and one week to prepare for the arrival of educators to work in their rooms. This would be my first opportunity to meet them. At this point, I was excited yet terrified at the same time. I was ultimately responsible for 220 students and 50 staff members. I was given a list of meetings that I would need to attend, to ensure: the budget was allocated, board policies were adopted and shared, understanding of the bullying policy, social media issues, harassment training, ALICE and Safe School training, CPI training, IEP training, as well as numerous other district initiatives that I had to implement. This was in addition to the visions I wanted to bring to my new school. After the excitement of the job somewhat dissipated, the reality of what was expected of me hit like a ton of bricks. I immediately went for the book by Todd Whitaker **What Great Principals Do Differently**. Throughout this book, I found numerous ideas of what I needed to do to improve areas of the school. The school I was inheriting was comprised of 100% free and reduced lunch students, 35% special education classes, three units of severely behavioral classes, and the average years of staff experience in education was less than seven years. Open staff positions were filled with long-term substitutes and non-licensed educators. Teachers were transferring out of the school, and I inherited a stack of student withdrawal requests to charter schools. I had to get involved and see why everyone was trying to leave the school I was just appointed to. As a principal in my district, you do not have control over who is placed in your building. This is an advantage at times but for me, coming with business experience, it is a problem I continually confront. I would like to be able to go to job fairs and recruit like-minded people for my school. If you have the chance to be a part of the educational hiring process, please take advantage of it. This is such a critical piece as it is hard to find qualified teachers, let alone qualified teachers who have the potential to be All-Stars.

2 PLANNING FOR SUCCESS

"Perseverance is not a long race; It is many short races one after another"
Walter Elliot

HUNTER'S PRINCIPAL PHASES OF LEADERSHIP DESIGN PROCESS

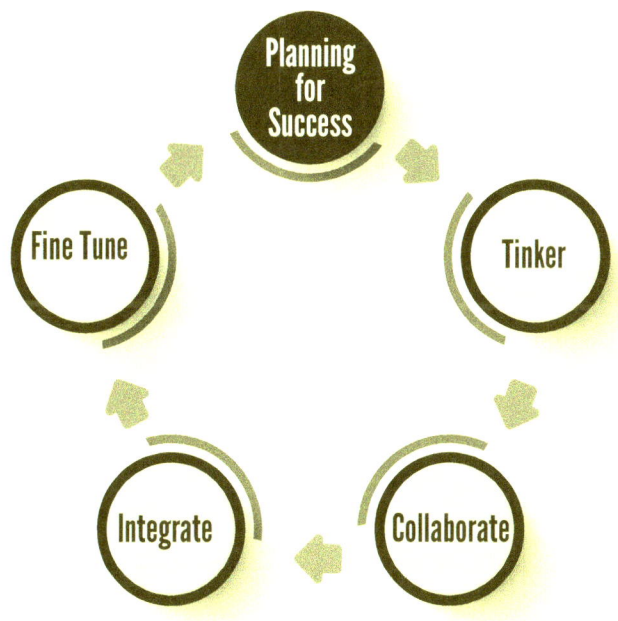

I developed this design framework to help beginning and veteran urban leaders organize how and when to implement change. Empirical change must happen with deliberate acts by leadership. By using this framework and collecting student data, you will set the foundation for your organization to grow exponentially. In each section of this book, if you follow this framework, it will assist you with making complex decisions for a successful and productive school year.

READY TO LEAD! THE BUILDING IS YOURS!

Let's Start with some Non-negotiables

Here is a short list of tasks that must be done regardless of any school system you work for:

1. Begin to build your 1st staff meeting presentation
2. Review all 504 and IEP plans
3. Review all safety and fire procedures and ensure they are up to date
4. Review all Union Contracts if applicable
5. Review all budgets and inventory with school purchase manager or secretary
6. Review purchase orders from the previous year to gauge what was purchased previously
7. Draft a welcome letter to your staff

Here are some key stakeholders as you start your role as an instructional leader and pertinent questions to guide your instructional leadership role.

This is a great opportunity to practice your skill of listening to the conversation.

1. School Secretary
2. Building Custodian
3. Food Service Manager
4. School Improvement Team
5. Assistant Principal or Dean of Students

SCHOOL SECRETARY

After you greet your secretary, schedule some time with him/her to go over the following questions and information:

1. What is the attendance procedure?
2. When is attendance due and how is it completed and tracked?
3. Do you have a current staff roster?
4. Who completes purchase orders for supplies?
5. How are visitors and volunteers admitted and vetted?
6. How are daily medicines distributed?
7. What is the registration process for new enrollees and for students leaving the school? Is the principal notified on either? (*I would recommend meeting every new family who registers and giving them a tour. Meet with every parent who chooses to unenroll to learn why they are leaving. These are important meetings to gauge what you need to improve on.*)
8. How are medically fragile students assisted?
9. How are 504's documented? Are copies placed in files? How are IEPs stored?
10. Locate the federal books on parents' rights under an IEP. Make sure they are accessible, as you will spend around 15% of your time in IEP meetings.
11. Ask your secretary who the key members are of the PTO.
12. Discuss if any grants are funded or are in process that needs to be completed.
13. Check if there is a teacher leader in the building.

BUILDING CUSTODIAN

1. How are the grounds patrolled and how is litter cleaned up?
2. What is the process to have something repaired? Does technology equipment fall under your jurisdiction? If not, then whom?
3. How do you notify the fire department when you are conducting a drill?
4. Are there any building safety issues that were not addressed and I need to be aware of?

These kinds of questions seem very basic; however, when you are tasked with opening a school, having this list handy will allow you to stay focused on your initiatives. The great thing about questions is that they lead to more questions.

Jeffrey J. Fox, the author of **How to Become a CEO** says, "Always be on the lookout for ideas. Be completely indiscriminate as to the source. Get ideas from all stakeholders, children, bus drivers, cab drivers, competitors and other industries. It doesn't matter who thought of the idea."

FOOD SERVICE MANAGER

1. How is the lunch count tallied each day?

2. What percentages of our students are on free and reduced lunch?

3. Are extra items for sale in the cafe? If so, what, and where does the money go to?

4. What works in your eyes as scheduling is concerned? (Very important to listen and not make any changes right away unless there are safety issues)

5. Are there any cafeteria safety issues that need to be addressed?

(Some principals spend two to three hours in the cafeteria. My assistant will spend some time monitoring. However, we empower our volunteers to handle the problems and support them when a situation arises. This allows me to continue as an instructional leader and not a manager of a cafeteria.)

SCHOOL IMPROVEMENT TEAM

This is a valuable relationship and one that needs to begin with a strong foundation. The majority of the time should be spent listening. I suggest asking the following questions:

1. Does the school have a School Improvement Team?
2. If so, who comprises the team?
3. What role do you play in providing or selecting professional learning for the staff?
4. Are there any safety issues that need to be addressed?
5. How is feedback and communication provided to the staff and stakeholder?

These are vague and simple questions; however, it will provide the necessary dialogue to establish a relationship. Once again, do much more listening than talking.

ASSISTANT PRINCIPAL

If you have an established assistant principal, please spend time getting to know him/her and be prepared to listen to how the school operates prior to your leadership. It is imperative to understand that assistant principals in the urban environments usually revolve around cafeteria duty and discipline. It is also vital that you treat your assistant principal as part of your School Improvement Team and that you agree with everything that both of you are going to be accountable for. As a principal, the instructional leadership piece should be at the focal point of every minute of your day. Empower your assistant to handle the things that allow you to be the instructional leader while still building capacity in your assistant's leadership style by him/her modeling your behaviors. It is essential to listen and get the pulse or mindset to see where assistant principals fit into your leadership style. Do not commit to change anything directly, just state that you are going to evaluate everything and appreciate his or her insight into the school. Make your own observations and evaluations of staff. Don't let hearsay have the power to sway your decisions. One of the first things I impress upon principals that I mentor, to form their own opinion on whom the effective educators are in their building. I stress the importance not to believe the statements from educators outside the school or former people who have their own agenda.

Questions to ask your assistant principal:

1. What is the morning arrival procedure?
2. How many buses arrive at school?
3. Do teachers have bus duties?
4. Who is responsible for monitoring the buses?
5. Who greets the students and where?
6. Are parents allowed to walk their child into school?
7. Are there hotspots in the school where fights or disagreements occur?
8. How often are suspensions used for safety infractions?
9. Do you currently track referrals or suspensions?
10. Are students allowed to go to the restroom by themselves or only with the class?
11. What is the process for a student being sent out of class?
12. Who handles discipline?
13. Are there any safety issues I need to be aware of?

MEET AND GREET YOUR STAFF

Meet with your staff in their rooms as they come in to work.

I send an introductory email to staff with a schedule of when the building will be open and when they can retrieve their classroom keys. This is an excellent time for a quick meet and greet, time to interact. I also make frequent trips to their rooms and carry their supplies for two reasons. The first reason is it allows me another non-confrontational interaction with conversation. I may get the opportunity to converse with the teacher in order to understand their educational philosophies. For example, I can ask a question about how they use their word wall, formula wall or ask what kind of seating arrangement they find most effective for the specific age group. If you listen carefully, you may catch a need or want that the teachers require. There are times, for example, when I have that item in storage and will bring it down for the educator to use. This is a small gesture to demonstrate that you are instructionally working as a facilitative leader. The second reason is it shows I am willing to assist and respect each educator. I value the mantra of being a servant to my educators. When educators see you as an extension of the classroom, it is easier for change initiatives to gain momentum. I want to use every available moment to build relationships with each staff member.

I spend a great deal of time reading educational materials and sources to ensure I stay current on all pedagogy and strategies. You must be an educational leader and be able to converse about topics that apply to your educators. You must also offer suggestions or new ideas on how they can improve in any area. An instructional leader needs to show excellent credibility when it's time for an observation or evaluation. By being well versed in research and evidence-based approaches to observations and walkthroughs, it helps provide credibility to your evaluation of them and allows it to be more of a coaching experience versus an evaluative experience. I firmly believe how important it is to read as much as you can on pedagogy in the areas you manage. When starting as an employee at a new school, people want to converse and tell you what works or doesn't work for them. I always find it helpful to rephrase the conversation using these simple questions, "How was the end of the year last year?" "Did you have a nice summer?" and "What is great about this school?" This is usually all that it takes, and you garner more information than you ever wanted. The final thing I always ask is, "Is the school safe for all parties involved?" Any of the former questions can be adapted depending on if this is your first year in the school or your fifteenth. The latter may seem like a simple question, but it is the one thing that can be a typical catalyst for change and a great way to show commitment to the staff.

In the business world, the new CEO of ALCOA Aluminum focused on the safety of his staff to build morale and to help empower the workers to make the company more profitable. No, we don't have the same goals as ALCOA. However, everyone wants to feel the leadership cares about them. An example of a statement from a teacher was, "I don't understand why we have to go to the gym during a tornado drill." I wrote down the concern and followed up with the security director and provided a response to the teacher. In this instance, she was right. It was a poorly designed plan and together we came up with a solution. This type of small victory produced instant credibility in her mind. I would also receive dozens of comments in regard to, "…too many students unsupervised in the halls and bathrooms." This was something I also documented, however, this needed to be a school decision, not a random issue easily resolved on a case by case basis. So, I discussed the comments with the School Improvement Team and jointly found a resolution. **My School Improvement Team consists of a mix of general education teachers and special education teachers.** The single most important idea I recommend, and continually do, is to share the leadership.

Shared Leadership is a new trend in education, and I will give some examples of how it works in the current capacity. In most businesses, all leadership is shared, or else you would be working in a micromanaged enterprise which will, most likely, not yield success. It is important that when you have an idea, you treat it as a sales opportunity. You need to be able to acquire support and buy-in from staff before you expect the initiative to work. I spent significant time selling my vision and showing the evidence and research behind why I think it is good practice for our school to move forward. I use the work and findings of John Hattie and Robert Marzano when I am pitching an idea. They have researched effect sizes of certain practices in schools. I will not ask my staff to complete a task or change practice unless the effect size yields an increase. It is also important not to give an opinion; it is important for you to only show the research and evidence, that what you are suggesting will increase student achievement. If you believe that you can force "your" initiative on the staff, you will be in for a long year.

Learning from the Great Navy Captain, Michael Abrashoff, "I vowed to treat every encounter with every person on the ship as the most important thing at that moment." It is important that as a leader, critical feedback given to educators is based upon actual evidence. Strategies also need to be provided in order to correct the deficient areas. Educators want their principal to be the leader and lead the organization by modeling their high expectations. They want to be led to a place and point that causes intrinsic motivation and the feeling of purpose in the organization. This cannot occur if you don't first listen and discuss things that both parties agree are important. That is why I chose safety over pedagogy or curriculum for the start of the school year as a principal.

As a new leader, you are looking for simple wins to build the culture of the building. Do not plan on going in and putting your "mark" on the school when you first arrive. Instead, watch, manage, and then begin to tinker around starting in January, unless there are safety issues that need to be addressed. I will discuss in the next chapter, step by step, the process of change under my paradigm chart.

MEETING WITH THE SCHOOL COMMUNITY

What's another critical factor that will help your school? Calling on the community. Throughout my first month, I was continually trying to determine if there were any community partners, sponsors or parents who were integrated into the school community. I made a list of all the churches in the school area and met with pastors/ministers. I informed them that I needed their insight and assistance as I had a desire to assist with turning the community around, focusing on student learning. I took copious notes on what were the most prominent issues: drugs, lack of food, lack of sports, illiteracy or other items. Every pastor I spoke with named all the items alone as equally present and essential to changing the community.

The next step during these weeks was to look at all the transfer requests that came into the school over the past two months. When I walked into the school, they were losing students to Charter schools rapidly, and it was the high performing students who were leaving. How was I ever going to change this building into a place where teachers, students, and parents want to come and learn?

Once I arranged and charted all the student transfer paperwork with addresses onto a map, the work began. I went door to door in the neighborhood and spoke with everyone in the household that was available about why they were leaving the school. I asked them to reconsider, some did, and some did not.

A few families did eventually come back once they saw the changes that were transpiring. I met more people that day walking the neighborhood, and I genuinely believe the neighborhood saw me as someone who cared about changing their children's futures. Always make sure, however, you feel comfortable in your surroundings before you embark on this adventure. I made it known that I was there to offer support and wanted stakeholders to feel welcomed in our school.

One of the great things about traveling and meeting people is the look on their face when you knock on their door. They assume you are selling something, however, when you introduce yourself, you have immediate credibility. I drop off a basic flyer about available after-school programs and I ask for parental support. I try to learn and remember as many names as possible. However, it is not the main focus. What is necessary is that you make them feel their child is essential and there is a place in their child's life at your school.

I was once told by a parent volunteer the following statement, "The reason why poor families don't like to come into the school is that they normally had bad experiences there and it brings back a stressful time." Maybe that is why we get such little parental attendance for events. We need to engage the community in ways they feel secure in coming to the school. Without their impact, the school never would have changed.

BUDGET AND FISCAL RESPONSIBILITY

If you are located in an urban environment, you most likely will have access to some federal funds. If you are not, you still will be provided with school improvement money or money from the general fund. If you do not have a strong background in finance, I suggest you ask the Director of Finance or one of his assistants to counsel you. You should also use the previous year's purchase records to gauge how much paper, supplies and other items were used. The most important question you can ask yourself prior to purchasing is, "Will this purchase help my students learn and be successful?" You must have fiscal responsibility and make every purchase in the eyes of the taxpayer. Would they be content with what you are purchasing? Always look throughout the school; you would be surprised how many supplies are stored in locations you would not think of. Ask the custodian if he/she knows of any "stashes."

Another way to generate funds that can be used for the "cutesy" things is through a PTO account or Student Activity Fund. Be aware, there have been numerous court cases on the embezzlement of PTO funds. I chose instead to have my district open an account for my school and have all monies run through the district. It is a pain at times to have a Purchase Order generated, however, neither I nor anyone else has access to the money once it is deposited. If you go the traditional route of PTO, make sure the PTO gets bonded and the checks require two signers. You must sit in on all PTO meetings and also try to recruit an educator or two. These PTO funds can be used for field trips, food, and activities that federal funds are listed as restricted purchases. Title One Funds are very clear on what they can be used to purchase. Make sure you check with your school's treasurer on percentage allocation and other metrics used for Title One Funds.

CUSTOMER SERVICE

The best way to start the year is to ensure your primary office has superb customer service. Your secretary should answer the phone in a professional manner and treat all staff members and parents with empathy and tact. This is something that you control immediately as you model appropriate behavior when parents come into the school. Welcoming them and introducing yourself shows how you want office staff to address parents and visitors. I remember in the book *212* **Leadership,** the quote, "Excellence is not a skill, it is an attitude." Few, if any skills are necessary to be courteous to visitors, students, and adults. We must treat all children with respect, as well. I have a zero yelling policy in my administration office and school. I make it known that yelling at a child will not be tolerated. Post this quote somewhere in your personal area, "It's your school. You are responsible for the results". The mindset of this statement is for you to continually look at the standards you have for yourself. No one is going to come to the school and have a difficult conversation with underperforming personnel. If you make that your mindset, the things that are needed to evaluate and slowly change the school will happen organically and with little unrest.

One of the things you can implement or reinforce immediately is that all calls must be returned within 24 hours to all parents or stakeholders. This also applies to emails. You want to do the majority of your communication via email. So, make it a priority that your staff checks email at a minimum of once per day. Do not assume these items are a given. They must be required and reinforced. Another great idea is to place a survey on the back of the monthly newsletter that parents can fill out and send back to the school. This gives them a non-confrontational approach to telling you what is working in their eyes, and what is not.

From my desk, I remember walking into my school and hearing the phones answered, "Chase STEMM Academy. This is (Insert Name)." I immediately changed this to, "Chase STEMM Academy. This is (Insert Name). How may I help you?" Something very similar but it changes the whole culture of the conversation. I also had to remind the secretary that when she was on the phone and someone walks in, it was not okay to ignore them or turn her back to them. A simple smile and acknowledgment will appease and make the visitor feel important; significant. These seem like common sense items but believe me, they are not prevalent in many of the schools I visit. Once again, make sure you model the proper required procedures. In the event comments are made from staff members, kindly remind them that our parents are accepted for who they are not what they may or may not do. They are our parents and every time we have an opportunity to meet with them, we can show them our safe and caring learning-centered school. **Each day, ask yourself how you can change someone's life.**

DESIGNING THE MASTER SCHEDULE

In middle and elementary schools, the schedule is more relaxed. I would look at transition times between classes, namely, reading and math blocks. Should they be longer? Ensure you listen to all stakeholders, but at the end of the day, you need to build a schedule that accommodates your learners and your school priorities. As a district, we have used ***schoolschedulingassociates.com***. This company is owned by Mr. Michael Rettig, and there are some free resources available on his website. There is an "art" to creating an effective schedule.

One other item that you should look at when you are building the schedule is how it was completed previously. My first year, I copied last year's schedule and just made a few minor changes due to additions and subtractions in staffing. This is a great idea instead of making changes when you're not sure what even works at this point.

FIRST STAFF MEETING

All the anticipation, the planning, the waiting; it is finally here, the first staff meeting! Your entire staff is looking at you and evaluating what kind of a leader you are and will be.

Cara Alter writes, "Credibility is not about having great ideas but, rather, about saying those ideas so that people will listen." **The Credibility Code** is a great book to read when you have time and are ready to practice your public speaking skills. Here is a list of non-negotiable points to practice to ensure you have credibility when you speak:

1. Make sure your hands stay in your gesture box. They should center right at the navel. Keep your hands present in that area from the beginning of your presentation.

2. Do not sway back and forth.

3. Head must remain level when speaking. Use your nose as a laser pointer toward a level spot on the wall. Move no more than every minute.

4. The faster you talk, the more nervous you appear.

5. Watch the movie **The Great Debaters** prior to first staff meeting.

6. Hold eye contact for 3-5 seconds, any longer is unnatural.

This is not a complete list of strategies. However, if you practice and use these few pointers when you give your presentations, it will give you greater credibility.

Your staff is waiting for your boring PowerPoint with a handout so they can peruse through and see what is going to change this year. I am not against PowerPoint or Prezi; however, do not place more than 7 words on a bulleted item. The PowerPoint should only consist of topics, not every word of your presentation. And don't, I repeat, **do not read from the PowerPoint**.

As teachers walk into the staff meeting, be sure to have a few songs playing. For example, if your meeting starts at 9:00AM, have your laptop set up playing 3 songs on a continuous loop. Some good music suggestions are Pop 40, Piano Guys or Pentatonix. Also, have a few pictures of your family or sports or hobbies on a slide show. This helps the staff know and understand you as a person.

Begin the staff meeting with a story before you introduce anyone or yourself. The story should be no more than five minutes and have relevance to the year ahead. My first story was taken from Jay Bilas' book ***Toughness***. It was a story about Sabrina Lewandowski, a 4th-grade teacher who had a brain tumor and was given a grim prognosis. The story has a happy ending and is an excellent segway into the emotion that everyone can relate to, *hope*. Spend time reading and speaking with people until you find the right story. Do not dismiss this tactic as this can help to frame your vision as a leader. A few pointers for storytelling:

1. Don't be the *hero* of your own story.
2. Tell stories from pictures.
3. All stories must have sensory details.
4. Remember that feelings are far more powerful than facts.

So, the story is over, and the audience is now engaged. This is a perfect time to introduce yourself and the staff members who are new to the building. Once the staff is introduced, make sure you go over the norms of the meeting. In future years, your School Improvement Team can collaborate and come up with school norms. For now, here is a list of some norms you should introduce:

1. Value each other's opinion
2. Limit side conversations
3. Limit the personal use of technology
4. For specific questions, please ask independently following the staff meeting.

Leaders can get easily discouraged when some staff members choose to not be engaged. I empower you to look past a few of the laggards and remember to put all your effort into your best people and you will yield improving results. I use a strategy to re-engage reluctant adult learners by briefly looking at them for 3-5 seconds as they are breaking that norm.

The norm that I find the most valuable is number four. There are so many times when you are in a meeting, and it is hijacked by one person who wants a specific answer to their specific classroom. This is not the appropriate time for that discussion, and you should merely state to that person that you can discuss that scenario after the meeting. You also want to make space for a "parking lot" where staff can leave questions, etc. When they use the parking lot, make sure to create a shared document and answer all of the items that were listed. A staff member took the time to write the question, make sure you answer it.

Next, you should review the school and district mission and the vision statement- ensure that everyone is aware of them. They should be posted and reviewed each day in classrooms as well as on the school announcements. If there is not a mission/vision statement, make this a priority with your staff for a future meeting.

This is a perfect time to practice safety drills. I would recommend that you lay out the procedures for school lockdowns, ALICE or any other active shooter practice scenarios your school or district uses. You want to make sure everyone understands where they are to go and how he or she is to communicate in the event of an active shooter. This is something that should be reviewed with your school or district safety department. It is imperative to have your staff practice these procedures before it is practiced with the students. Discuss Fire Safety Week and inform school personnel that you will be doing drills at least once a month. I advise for elementary students performing two a month at the beginning of the year and not undertaking as many during the winter, especially in northern areas. It just makes sense to practice the first few months of school, so the students are prepared in the event of an issue. I am also a strong advocate for the use of red/ green clipboards to ensure safety, especially during drills. They can be purchased. A current class list and medication instructions list should be placed on the clipboard at all times. Once an alarm bell rings, every educator should grab the clipboard for their class, take attendance, and then hold up green for 100% attendance or red for missing a student. This will allow you, as an administrator, to get an immediate assessment if students are missing or in harm's way.

The next step for staff meetings is to display a video or read a book that lasts 4-5 minutes on a topic that is important to you as a change agent:

I chose to read **Mrs. Spitzer's Garden** by Edith Pattou. It is a book about how important teachers are to their students and how we all have to add to our tool chest to be the best we can be.

Here is a list of a few more literacy selections for future staff meetings:

- **Alexander and the Terrible, Horrible, No Good, Very Bad Day**: This teaches how to be proactive; how could we handle bad scenario's better

- **The Little Red Hen**: How everyone wins when everyone helps

- **Pout Pout Fish**: Being Proactive and choosing your own mindset

- **Ada Twist Scientist**: Inquiry

- **Conversation Club**: How to work in groups

These are just a few of the videos I prefer and am always adding more videos to my twitter feed:

- ***Keeper of the Flame**, YouTube*
- ***The Tree Lead*** from India
- Videos by ***The Pipe Guy***

Now that you have gathered staff attention, it is important to review the previous year's State Test Data and discuss any improvement that can be a focus for this school year. Only use this data as a "carrot", or reward, to continue to improve student learning. This should be a very high-level analysis. Pair teachers by grade level and provide the following guiding questions:

DATA DEVELOPMENT QUESTIONS

1. Has an in-depth and comprehensive analysis of the student performance data been conducted?
2. Does the data provide a comprehensive and accurate reflection of the overall performance of students? Did you review subgroup data?
3. Could your school clearly describe the strengths and limitations of students' learning based on the data you have collected?
4. Is most staff involved in the improvement process?

INTERACTION MAY LOOK LIKE THIS:

Principal: "We did a great job with our subgroup of African American males, they improved by 4%. That's great growth. We always want to set our goals high, and it looks like 7% is within reach. I cannot wait to get started building on the success."

It is also essential to discuss discipline infractions. If data is not collected on a daily basis, now is the time to introduce that idea to the staff. Discuss how a behavior management system can allow you to minimize the distractions that occur in the school. Advise staff that this data will be collated at the administration level and shared with the staff in an anonymous way to improve behavior management. I will share in the next chapter, a successful behavior management tracking system.

This should also be the time you turn over the meeting to your assistant principal to discuss more procedural discipline items with staff members. During this time, take a seat and attentively watch your assistant, modeling how you should listen when in a meeting. Do not check your cell phone, email, or make calls in the office. You need to demonstrate that you are not better than or more important than anyone else in that meeting.

The remainder of the meeting should focus on housekeeping items and reminders. Review new Board Policies such as harassment policies, bloodborne pathogen policy training, and social media policies. How will data be shared with you? Will you utilize **Google** to communicate via **Calendar, Docs**, and **Sheets**? Will you use **Office 365**? Or will you use a product like **Dropbox**? Your goal should be to use as little paper as possible as it will allow you to work from anywhere there is an Internet connection. **Google Classroom** or a like kind of product, will also allow you to provide all data, forms, and items to your staff when they need them. It will minimize the emails or questions you get on items that do not raise your students' aptitude. For example, I receive frequent emails asking questions that could be answered by a FAQ type of program. Having all the forms, procedures and ideas in a shared folder, online, allows staff to review information and ask you implementation questions on how this can or will help with student achievement. Another example of frequent emails is requesting a copy of the master schedule. This was placed in a shared folder so everyone can view it prior to the start of the year and, as soon as possible, to allow collaboration amongst educators. Simple procedures save time and energy for all staff members.

You may feel like a great leader by giving your staff the forms they need, but you are doing nothing to help the students graduate or push the staff to become more engaged in their content pedagogy.

I always end my staff meeting with a lesson on **Growth Mindset** by Carol Dweck. This is a book that is a must-read. I discuss and give specific examples of what a growth mindset and a fixed mindset are and then ask everyone to focus on ways we can get the most out of each other and our stakeholders this year. Carol Dweck defines a fixed mindset as, "A fixed mindset, people believe their basic qualities, like their intelligence or talent, are simply fixed traits. They spend their time documenting their intelligence or talent instead of developing them. They also believe that talent alone creates success—without effort. They're wrong."

Dweck further states as a definition for a growth mindset, "In a growth mindset, people believe that their most basic abilities can be developed through dedication and hard work—brains and talent are just the starting point. This view creates a love of learning and resilience that is essential for great accomplishments. Virtually all great people have had these qualities."

We all have to believe that learners have the ability to learn the content as long as we provide it in the correct modality for them to learn and understand. I will provide more specific neuroscience information and how I use it in my current school.

I use stories, such as this one... I received a call from the Director of Pupil Placement in August of my second year as a principal. We started to change the climate of the building slowly or at least, righted the ship. The Director of Pupil Placement asked me if she could place a student, who has been thrown out of multiple schools, at my school for the next year. I immediately said yes and allowed Chet (not real name) to come to our school. I was warned by other principals to check his record or check the attendance of every student who tried to transfer in for that matter. I have never done this. Our job is to change children's lives, and we cannot expect them to come to us knowing how we expect them to behave. This was a learning curve for Chet and I. I met with him and advised him of our expectations and that he would have a new start here. There were many rough bumps along the way. He was arrested in early September for breaking into someone's home; he would get "high" on drugs after school, run the streets at night and sleep in school. We were not reaching him. I spoke with his ELA teacher, to come up with a solution. She said that she was developing a relationship with him and would build upon that. Chet might have been late to school, but he always came. Sometimes he was reeking of marijuana and sometimes with clothes unwashed. However, we all agreed we are not here to judge, we are here to educate. We took the proper protocols to notify his parents & child services, and we knew that real change had to come from Chet, himself. We could only be the catalyst for the change.

After much struggle, both academically and behaviorally, I am pleased to announce that Chet moved his Reading Test score from a 1 out of 5 to a 3 out of 5, rating him now *proficient*. Now, we all like stories where students go from 1 to a 5 but that is not scalable and is the outlier. We should study the outlier but not expect it to be a realistic goal for every single student immediately. Chet went on to finish 8th grade with a 2.6-grade point average and had zero suspension days. He had the opportunity to go to high school and be the first in his family to graduate.

Stories like this are everywhere and non-proprietary to my school. However, it all starts with focusing on what the children of our community need. They need someone to believe in them, and they all need an advocate for their education. This is an example of a perfect story of a child with a fixed mindset and adults with a growth mindset who changed him. Thus, changing Chet's life for that time period.

SUMMARY OF STAFF MEETING

The staff meeting is one of the oldest meetings that principals are required to organize. The first staff meeting, for me, sets the tone for the entire school year so that the remaining staff meetings can be used for professional learning. Once the tone of your leadership is set, you can communicate via email, **YouTube**, and other media to ensure that staff time is used to improve student and teacher performance. The first staff meeting is one that cannot be replaced by an email. That is why I made a specific point to focus on credibility, the tone of voice, and content. The staff's opinion about you will be formed within the first 15 seconds. I would also encourage you to look through videos, books and other platforms to find items that will stimulate conversations and lead to useful stories that can be told.

One final safety measure is set up a profile for the teachers on **remind.com**. I provide a copy of instructions to join the text service in every teacher's mailbox prior to the 1st day of school. This allows a quick and efficient medium to provide information to staff in a crisis situation.

Good luck with your first staff meeting and the beginning of the change process at your school.

SMALL CHANGES YOUR FIRST FEW WEEKS

I remember one of the first things I did when I started at my school. Every time I saw garbage on the floor, I would pick it up. Soon, I noticed that students began to pick up trash and show me as I walked by. Even middle school students, whom most people view as uninterested, were the biggest helpers. Another small but powerful cultural change was removing the black marks, made by certain types of shoes, off the laminate floor in the hallway. I would stop and remove the black marks by rubbing the sole of my shoe back and forth, so the hallways were clean. Not only did students love joining in to help, they also enjoyed the smile on the custodian's face. Her time now could be spent helping to make the bathrooms tolerable. Middle School students can really smell up a bathroom!

THREE MAIN POINTS THAT HELPED CHANGE THE CULTURE OF THE SCHOOL AND REMOVE THE SUSPENSIONS:

1. Greet every single student, every single day, when they walk into the building.
2. If there is any chance you can meet with parents on positive interactions, take advantage of them. Parent's perception of the school yields better-behaved children.
3. Let educators know that your office is an extension of the classroom. You will be in classrooms all the time to ensure effective instruction is occurring and that the learners understand the importance of the instruction.

What helped me achieve these three main points was listening to a speaker at a conference in 2015. After hearing Baruti Kafele speak, I knew the mantra that he spoke of fit perfectly into my school. "The students would be better simply because I was their educational leader." Mr. Kafele stated that if you don't believe this, you are not ready to lead students. Since 85% of the students in our school community are from single-family homes, I needed to be the steady, consistent voice in their lives. Parents are faced with so many obstacles and they may not have enough time to handle everything life throws at them. Schools need to partner with parents to focus on the needs of the students. Since I was raised by a single mom for part of my life, the number of items single parents must manage grows daily. I insist educators understand that once our learners step onto our property, it is up to us to ensure all learning takes place. I greet every single student each day and make sure they are in dress code. They do not get past me if their shirts are untucked or are wearing jeans or inappropriate T-shirts.

I simply had to take the school back from the students.

I spend 60% of all my time either in the hallways or in classrooms. During every transition, I am present correcting behavior and addressing the needs of the staff. When I visit classrooms, I ensure students are not sleeping and are paying attention and completely engaged. Now, whoever was not engaged, I would simply squat down next to them and quietly let them know my expectations if they were going to be in my school.

SUMMARY OF PLANNING FOR SUCCESS

I could write an entire book on how to prepare for the first six months of school. However, I want to delve more into the change process and give you insight into pedagogical changes, interacting and recruiting stakeholders and developing a school culture which yields success. Just to recap:

1. Make sure you have a full understanding of school educational standards on teacher effectiveness before you observe staff members.
2. If you inherit a school where the leader managed by fear and disciplinary write-ups, you should take a step back and form your own opinions. I challenge you to not read what your predecessor stated and form your own opinions.
3. Start with looking at small changes to make the school run more customer oriented.
4. If you can master these few steps along with documenting your staff's habits and the functionality of the school, it will help as we get into the **Tinker** stage.
5. I have used *remind.com* as an emergency notification system for parents to be notified in case of an immediate threat. I provide enrollment instructions for the service in the first school newsletter. There are other text services, however, I have found *remind.com* very user friendly and reliable.

3 TINKER

"You can spend your time at school however you choose, but you can only spend it once."
Ron Clark

HUNTER'S PRINCIPAL PHASES OF LEADERSHIP DESIGN PROCESS

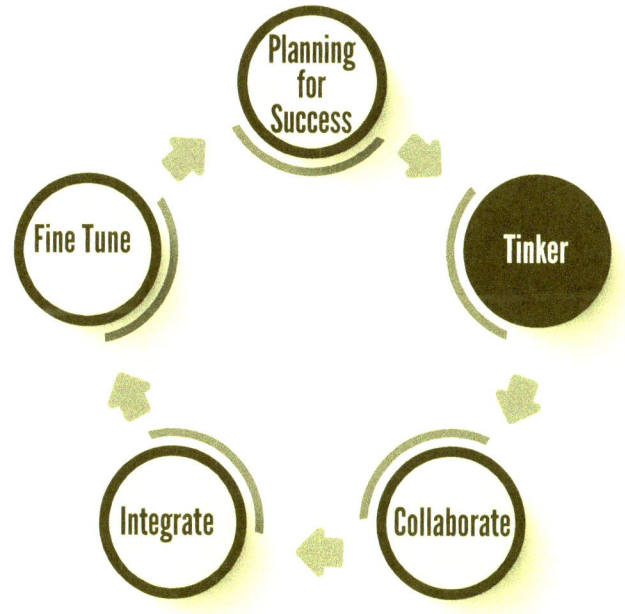

Why choose a word such as Tinker? This is where you make calculated small changes that can yield significant results. It is also when you start to change the culture and expectations of your building.

"If you want to see it, you have to teach it." When I visited Ron Clark's fabulous school in Atlanta, GA, a few of his statements stood out to me. "You can spend your time at school however you choose, but you can only spend it once." This resonated with me, and I made it my passion to take every moment possible to uplift someone, show someone how to demonstrate empathy for others and help change the lives of students academically as well as emotionally. Another powerful statement Mr. Clark said was, "My intent is to treat everyone fairly, but I am not going to treat everyone equally." This was also a notable quote to remember in the fields of education where people's salaries increase based on years served rather than on evidence-based improvement. Ron also goes on to mention that, as a leader, you need to make sure you impress upon your staff that you do not need to be someone's sponge for negativity. You will find negative teachers, administrators, parents, and students. "Do not be their sponge," was the message he was impressing upon us. Choose to see the glass as half full instead of half empty.

"A rising tide lifts all boats." If we change the culture slowly from the inside out by modeling what should occur, everyone is lifted organically. When students help to lead the change initiative, it is less about your movements and more about what is best for students. I spend time during lunch tutoring students in my office. I also spend 35% of my day in classrooms working with students and giving thumbs up to hardworking staff. You noticed I said working with students, not observing practitioners. If educators are to honestly show their "art" of teaching, then they first need to feel their time and conversations with the administrator are in safekeeping with the utmost confidence.

Without that type of mutual support, you will not be able to fully understand or view all the strengths of the staff. You need to be able to maximize the strengths and attributes of all staff members to fit the mission statement of the school. These are small ways to start the ripple and **Tinker**.

SCHOOLS HAVE NEVER SUSPENDED THEMSELVES INTO GREATNESS!

"Discipline is not punishment; Discipline is doing the right thing at the right time, to the best of your ability."- Jay Bilas. Correcting children and young adults is vital to the cultural changes you want to occur. The students do not run the school, you do. The teachers are looking for you to be fair and consistent with consequences. If you are not in charge of discipline, then make sure you have spent time working with your deans and assistant principals to go over your expectations. Suspensions are not the answer to problems. **Schools have never suspended themselves into greatness!** That is just putting a blanket over a problem. Discipline will change students' mindsets. They need to understand why the behavior or choice they made is not beneficial to their growth and to the growth of others involved. There are many educational theories and behavior management programs available. I currently use two programs and took it upon myself to combine pieces of both to create a perfect system for my school. I have used *Love and Logic* and *Restorative Justice*. These are frameworks that fit into PBS or PBIS which so many schools are working under the direction of. I am a firm believer that you discipline students while still showing them dignity and respect. And yes, it can be done, even when they are on your last nerve.

BEHAVIOR MANAGEMENT TRACKING DATA SYSTEM

SWIS is very cost effective and can provide granular data on the infractions. If you are unable to purchase data programs, a shared Excel template is a great way to start. Before I had the funding to use *SWIS*, I merely created an Excel template and tracked by educator, student, infraction location, and disposition. This allowed me to see where the trouble spots were and the time of day the incidents occurred. For example, I was able to see that the majority of classroom referrals occurred right after lunch when music class was taking place. Having this concrete data allowed me to provide support for the music specialist. The support included providing different classroom management strategies and professional development on behavior management. In addition, the administrative team knew what time to stop into specific classrooms to show support for the educators. I am a firm believer, as a leader, you can either go to the problem area and help prevent issues or you can sit in your office and wait for the problem to be sent to you after it already occurred. It is critical to be consistent with discipline, and it is also essential to provide feedback to the educators on which behaviors require referrals and which ones can be handled in alternate manners. Here again, this is not the time to discuss the teachers' deficiencies, merely a way to advise them that data will be tracked to improve the culture of the building and keep students in school and in class. The fewer times students are out of the classroom waiting for a consequence, the more time they could spend in their classrooms learning. We use this data to see where we can improve procedures. For instance, if there are a lot of bathroom issues after recess, educators and I collaborate to try and remedy the situation and come up with some ideas or strategies. The data allows us to focus on improvement versus blaming someone for not doing a great job managing the children.

1ST YEAR DATA DIVE

With the advent of the common core and the new testing metrics, the scores of almost all schools within our district had dropped significantly. In my current district, schools that always received an "A" on their school report card, dropped to a "C" or lower. The studies that took place under the previous state testing metrics were no longer valid in the era of "The Common Core or Higher State Standards." Even states that did not adopt the common core, increased the rigor in their standards, which caused the scores of schools to drop and force the districts to find interventions and solutions to increase standards. The AIR, PARCC and other state-mandated tests have increased the rigor of assessments that are given to the students. This caused educators to look for ways to improve the rigor of their instruction.

By making data comparisons of schools of similar size and similar demographics, this gave me the baseline I needed to improve student performance. I would use this data as a motivational tool for the hard work we were doing as the results were showing improvement. We had documented successful formative assessment data. However, schools are judged on the summative assessments from the previous years. During the data conversations with staff, I spent more time during the meetings asking questions. John Maxwell, in his book ***Good Leaders Ask Great Questions*** states, "Good questions inform; great questions transform." My concept was to transform the thinking of instruction without it being my idea. I was hoping to create capacity in the staff to be self-motivated change agents. My goal is for each staff member to be the best in their pedagogy. I used various educational articles from ***Education Week*** and other sources on the Internet to stimulate thinking among the staff.

Data Wall

As a first year principal, I felt it was important to convey to the staff that I was aware of our formative and summative data of the school. ALAS! The invention of my Data Wall. I wanted to share everything that was happening in our school with all stakeholders and make it a focal point and conversation piece with staff and students. I took a vacant wall in the main hallway and changed the name to *Mr. Hunter's Data Wall*. I began with very simple data comparisons, such as:

1. Previous Year State Report Card Results (by grade)
2. Current Number of Suspension Days
3. Current Attendance Rate and Goal
4. School Mission and Vision
5. Any school wide formative assessment charts, such as, DIBELS, Map Projections, STAR projections or other school-wide growth initiatives.

I created these items on poster paper and laminated them so the data could be seen as part of a growth mindset. I would update weekly and make sure everyone owned the data. *(Always make sure the names of students and teachers are not present. This ensures confidentiality and ensures it is a growth activity).*

SCHOOL IMPROVEMENT TEAM

I actually used this specific activity, explained above, with my School Improvement Team to gather data for our School Improvement Plan. We collected information on content domains which our students were struggling with. We then dissected the data in order to identify any gaps in the curriculum. Once the School Improvement Team noticed a few "gray" areas within the curriculum, we built our professional learning around improving writing in each classroom.

After the collation of all data, student samples, and summative assessments, my staff and I agreed that we needed to improve our writing instruction. It was extremely valuable to have all the data projected onto a line graph to see where improvements needed to be made in each domain. After studying the linear line, a discussion followed about how and why some students excelled while others did not perform well. Some of the issues that were discovered were poor student conventions, low vocabulary acquisition and lack of understanding of author's voice/purpose. This data allowed us to look at different and improved methods to improve writing instruction and also implement for the following school year.

I always use this quote when staff and I begin an intensive project, or as I like to describe it, "some heavy lifting". "You can study gravity forever without learning how to fly," Sean Achor. Mr. Achor, in ***The Happiness Advantage,*** discusses how we need to study the outlier, not the average. It does not mean we should expect all students to become the outlier. Instead, examine deeper to discover what information one learner saw differently than the others during instruction. Achor also uses an analogy from a TV commercial, "4 out of 5 dentists recommend ____ toothbrush." Well, what does the one dentist know that the four who endorse the product do not?

FOCUS

At this stage of the process, the students should know who you are and what you stand for. In studies, the 90/90/90 schools and the book by Cathy Lassiter, ***The Simple Truths of High Performing School Cultures,*** which I am a firm believer in, stated the top 5 things that school leaders must focus on:

1. Laser Focus on Student Achievement
2. Clear Curriculum Choices
3. Frequent assessments and multiple opportunities for improvement
4. Emphasis on nonfiction writing
5. Collaborative scoring of student work

When I was tasked with changing my current school from a culture where all teachers worked in "silos", to a more collaborative environment, I knew I had to find a way where we all could improve together. As there was little, if any, creative instruction; collaboration; innovation; or imagination among the group of educators, I chose to tackle writing as the crux of the change process. Writing is something that is easy to introduce and is cross-curricular and self-differentiates. When I first asked teachers to really push writing, I gave little direction as I was in the **Tinker** stage. I took notes on which strategies teachers used with students. Did they use Collins Writing, 6-Traits, and graphic organizers or just free write? Did they work on building stamina or just gave the students prompts or topics? It was not crucial at this stage; I just wanted to see how they instructed the students to write.

My suggestion to you is to start giving your educators little hints on writing. At a staff meeting, I would pose the following questions and ask staff members to write a response:

- **Question:** Why do we exist as an institution?
- **Question:** Is the school currently the best it can be? Why or Why not?

I would pose these questions and have staff answer them and either share in a small group or just have a brief discussion about the presented questions. Once that metaphoric wall of apprehension is broken down, it is a great time to have a whole group open discussion on the extended response questions and how answers pertain to the importance of assessments. Discuss how the entire staff can take a multidisciplinary focus on writing for the remainder of the year. I inherited fragmented teacher groups who met irregularly and with little oversight. I knew a change was needed.

STAFF EVALUATIONS

Michelle Akers, a former US Women's soccer player, states, "Don't mistake routine for commitment." Many times, principals delightfully share whom they had to "write up" or who are the troublemakers. I find it integral to form my own opinions and will kindly place those teacher records in a box and store them in a locked storage closet. School transformation is the outcome of individual transformation. In most businesses, you inherit people that were not hired by you. In this instance, most likely, none of your staff will be hired by you. Do not expect them to be loyal to you and like you just because you are the principal. If you continue to focus on safety and slowly place an extreme emphasis on customer service and professionalism, that will weed out many issues.

As you start evaluations, it is crucial that you study and research what each *standard* looks like in the classroom. I always start my evaluation by looking for the learning target in the classroom. Having the learning target notated on the board is nice but what is more telling is if the instruction relates to the target. If the learning targets do not relate to the instruction, then that is a big area of concern. Thus, the students have no idea why they are learning the material.

I used the following resources to assist with evaluations. I have read dozens of books including ***The Power of Habit*** by Charles Duhigg, ***The Happiness Advantage*** by Sean Achor, and ***Gung Ho*** by Ken Blanchard. I would also recommend the books that are listed below. As a leader, you should continue to read and learn along with your staff. My goal is to read at least two books per month on topics that will assist me as a leader and an instructional leader/coach. This is a great starting point for you. Educators are professionals and demand an evaluation by a competent evaluator. This will increase your credibility and also improve the instruction in their classroom by offering professional ideas or strategies by other authors. Always remember that you want to start every conversation and end every conversation with something positive.

BOOKS I WOULD RECOMMEND USING:

1. ***Qualities of Effective Teachers*** by James Stronge
2. ***Thoughtful Classroom Program***
3. ***Research-Based Methods of Reading Instruction*** by Sharon Vaughn and Sylvia Thompson
4. ***Administrator's Guide to Interpreting the CCSS to Improve Math*** (Even if the CCSS does not apply, the state standards are very similar.)
5. Use ***The Teaching Channel***
6. Check your individual state's website for model curriculum and teaching standards. Training is available at most state levels to assist with scripting evaluations and applying them to a rubric. However, if no training is available, look for district-approved or school-approved evaluations.

My favorite book is ***The Happiness Advantage*** by Shawn Achor. In this book, Achor spends a lot of time giving ideas on why happiness is missing from enterprises and how a happy workforce is a productive one. This is a must-read for any educator and leader.

It is essential to give only one refinement and one reinforcement per evaluation with an educator. It is too difficult to concentrate and make changes on multiple issues.

Positive Change Movement

Our School Improvement Team decided that if we were going to make the school a happy place, we needed to start a positive change movement. We formed a book study around ***The Happiness Advantage***. We met weekly, discussed each chapter, and came to the realization that sometimes the problem was not the students. The author goes on to state that the mean age for depression fifty years ago was 29.5 years old. Today, it is almost half of what it was fifty years ago. The average age when depression starts now is 14.5 years old. Another example shows that doctors who were put into a positive mood prior to making a diagnosis resulted in almost three times more intelligence and creativity than doctors in a neutral state, and made accurate diagnosis 19 times faster. This data easily translates to schools; we know that when a student is happy, and dopamine is released inside the child, we have a happier and more engaged learner to instruct. Another strategy we use for standardized tests, again involves Mr. Achor.

His view is, "Students were told to think about the happiest day of their lives right before taking a standardized achievement test. Those students outperformed their peers." Positive psychology and collaboration is an integral part of changing the culture of your school. We may not have all the answers and can't directly change people's habits, however, we can make them think. Try to make someone think today about something positive or a goal you know they can reach. **Change Lives! Chose to be a Leader!!**

FINDING OR DEVELOPING TEACHER LEADERS

The questions I encounter the most while speaking with my peers and meeting principals from all over the country are, "How do you find teacher leaders?" "Do they volunteer?" "Are they born with "IT"?" and "Can you make a high performing teacher a leader?" The easy answer is yes and no. It is tough to find All-Star teachers or as Robyn Jackson says, "High Will/High Skill" teachers. I have found that most high performing educators work in silos and normally focus on their world or classroom. They normally do not volunteer to become leaders; it's normally the educators who are weak in instruction but strong in discipline that stand out to people as leaders. It is completely the opposite for me. I look at the fact that a teacher leader must have "high skill" and in the right environment, can transform into "high will" leaders. I use data to recruit leaders and also retain buy-in from staff on why this person is on our School Improvement Team. I also conduct a personality test with all staff members and find leaders with "high skill/high will" from every domain of the personality metric. This way the entire school is represented and each person has a like-minded peer they can relate to. I have found this to be a great way to get my agenda passed while showing transparency. I want to have all different kinds of leaders representing our School Improvement Team. Anthony Muhammad calls his high achievers "The Believers." He states that he asks his "…believers to engage with people in other paradigms." This is only effective as long as the leader is prepared to do so. Many times it takes months of practice to ensure the conversation that will be shared is safe.

I always challenge teacher leaders to improve their individual practices by offering them books that empower their creative and entrepreneurial spirit.

LEADERSHIP SIDE NOTE

As you begin to hone your leadership style under the **Tinker** Stage, pay close attention to the personal brand you are creating. You are slowly becoming an instructional leader. If you are following this guide, you are not becoming a manager. **You are becoming a forward thinker who will make positive changes in the entire environment!** A very distinct way to create your brand is to decide how you will present yourself. Your grooming habits and wardrobe will be what people see first when you enter any room or event. These choices will represent who you are and people will create an image by your appearance. What image will you display?

I have always found that when I needed to command attention, for example, giving a speech, I always wear black and grey or black and white. Avoid wearing bright colors when providing professional learning or at speaking engagements. You want to be a person who is open and concerned in those situations, not one who is power hungry. Bright colors are power colors (represented in your necktie or suit pocket square), and you want the power to be in your listeners when you are speaking, not in your accessories.

Another point is to be concise when sending emails. The wordier the emails, the more open you are to ridicule, either from people behind the scenes or from your staff members. Be polite and concise and let your teacher leaders discuss the ambiguous parts with their counterparts.

One final note as you work on your leadership and communication style, remember these statistics:

- Impact Words 7%
- Vocal Reflection and Words 38%
- Body Language 55%

Body language has the most impact for a speaker. It is essential to keep your hands in the speaker's box around your belly and make small movements, no more than every 30 seconds or so. You can physically move no more than once per minute and make sure you make eye contact for 3-5 seconds with your audience.

SUMMARY OF TINKER

The phrase "Disruptive Innovation" is being coined in educational circles all around us. I like the phrase and associate *innovation* with being able to view a problem and then finding a creative way to motivate people to solve that problem. The benefits of solving problems alone are few. Motivate your staff to solve problems collaboratively. What's the result? Innovation that disrupts the status quo. "The first step to wisdom is awareness." This embodies **Tinkering** to a "T". First, be aware of the issue at hand. Next, motivate with subtle changes. This can create excitement as collaboration continues about a possible solution. Ultimately, the problem can now be resolved by staff because there is motivation to drive that desire to make a change.

Before we delve into the chapter on collaboration, here is an example about how working collaboratively can impact student achievement. After the first quarter, my School Improvement Team and I noticed that in 3rd through 5th-grade, students were struggling immensely with fractions. Instead of blaming the students, parents or curriculum, we included the 3rd-5th-grade teachers in a work session to discuss how each teacher taught fractions to the students. As it turned out, all were using different terminology and different strategies. Some of the strategies were not even grade-relevant. In response, we disrupted the status quo. We began looking for mathematical texts that were more rigorous and trained each teacher on that specific pedagogy. We noticed over the next year, the scores in the fraction domain increased a few points. In addition, the attitude of our learners increased tremendously toward fractions.

    We know this will take time to scale and the scores will follow due to the hard work my staff did to improve this content area. When this happens, true innovation can occur, and staff will implement the ideas of the School Improvement Team. At the end of the day in education, we really don't have our own ideas, we just all share what we know is in the best interest of students.

4 COLLABORATE

"We cannot solve our problems with the same level of thinking that created those problems"
Albert Einstein

HUNTER'S PRINCIPAL PHASES OF LEADERSHIP DESIGN PROCESS

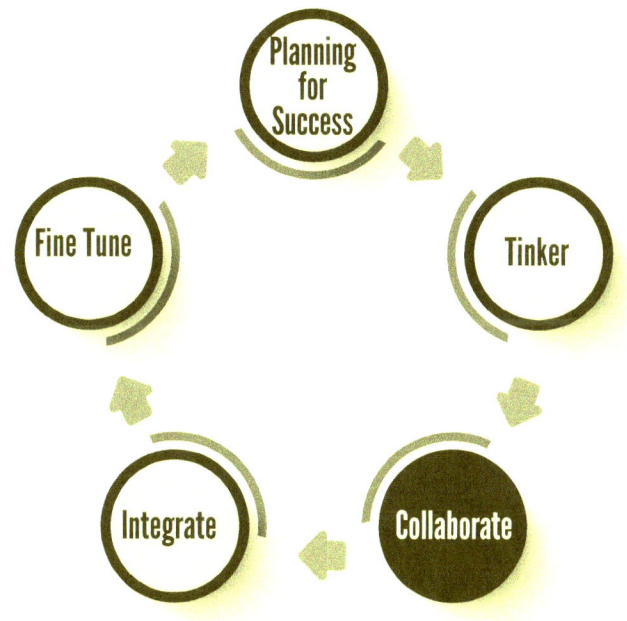

Now, only small but calculated changes have occurred. It is time to make your move and put your own mark on your building, right? Hold tight for one more minute. The first thing you should do is include your School Improvement Team in the change process. Even if you have fantastic ideas, you will get much further if your team has awesome ideas to share, as well. An essential piece to understand is that no matter what you implement, be prepared for only 80% buy-in, on the high side. You will always have people who are apathetic.

One-point that Richard Koch states in his numerous publications are to focus on the 80%, not the bottom 20% of your organization. The 20% can consume you like a sponge, but the 80% can move your school to the goal of a complete turn-around. Anthony Muhammed states, "What is more important, the proper cultivation of a child or being validated by your colleagues?" The school-based decision is not easy and sometimes requires difficult times, keep the focus. Muhammed goes on to say, "Culture represents the unwritten mission of the school." It tells students and staff why they are here. It is your responsibility now to ensure that the culture of the school moves in the right direction.

Depending on your situation and grade levels, collaboration may look different. If you are a leader in a small school with only one of each grade level, you will have to introduce vertical grade level groups. In this instance, I would have the two closest grades work together so they can share common assessments and view student samples. I usually insist that my music teacher work with the 3rd-5th-grade teachers as music is a significant catalyst to teach fractions. I focused my PE instructor on measurement with all grades but explicitly working with my K-2 learners. The art instructor would focus on geometry in the middle grades. If, however, you are the leader of a large school and you have at least two of each grade level, then I would have those instructors of the same grade level plan and create interventions together.

PROFESSIONAL LEARNING COMMUNITIES (PLC'S)

The term PLC's (Professional Learning Communities) has been around for years and has many different acronyms. PLC's are structured meetings between educators with a definitive goal. This can occur in vertical or horizontal grade bands. The most important components are the conversations that occur about improving student's achievement. As a leader, it is critical that you stress the importance of communicating across subject areas. Also, the data from these meetings can assist with the professional learning that is needed at your school.

As the year begins, I always work with the School Improvement Team to give the PLCs a starting point. We will look at summative data from last year's state tests and document what areas need our attention. I give each group a topic to start the meeting, ask them to do the following tasks, and then provide the information to the School Improvement Team when completed:

1. Complete the PLC information form. (There are numerous templates on the Internet and in PLC publications)
2. Decide when and where PLC's are going to meet. Must be consistent day and time so you can schedule to sit in and observe.
3. Use the data from the previous year's state tests, as no formative data is available, and then create the learning target for the first cycle of the PLC.
4. A typical PLC cycle should encompass around 4 weeks of instruction with a post assessment determining the success.

5. How will teachers know if the students need intervention or acceleration? *Intervention* in our PLCs is defined as working with students who are struggling with current standards or standards from previous grades. *Acceleration* in our PLCs is defined as educators pre-teaching complex items for deeper understanding. Accelerated content is instructed to learners who have already met mastery for the standard. The PLCs must look at samples of student work as the means for determining student mastery.

My educational background reminded me of Dufor's Professional Learning Communities and how this structure would be a great beginning for effective group work. As a small group or PLC , pose questions for students and find or develop a rubric for grading. Professional Learning Communities was created by Richard DuFour as a means for each group to collaborate and to share best practices. As Dufour writes, "PLCs are not a program. It is a framework of collaborating ideas with stakeholders of the same general grade band." It is very important that as a leader, you don't allow the ambiguous notion of discussion drive the time in your PLCs. You want to ensure that your PLCs are looking at actual student samples that the learners have completed. Once you have student work samples discussed in the PLC and decide what a high-quality paper is, base all other papers off of this representative sample. Discuss, as a group, the strengths and the weakness of the students. For example, if you notice all students struggled with a specific question on a formative assessment, spend time breaking the question down into parts within your PLC. The PLC should not be a regurgitation of information, yet a planning period for any gaps in instruction the data is presenting to the group. When a group has become proficient in this practice, it is vital that they share this information with their peers in other grades. I also suggest showing this information at the next staff meeting. As Dufor states, PLC structure is perpetual!

NORMS OF COLLABORATION

Our school uses some of the adaptive schools strategies, specifically, the norms of collaboration. These strategies created make a lot of sense as a framework for PLC's (Professional Learning Communities):

1. Pausing
2. Paraphrasing
3. Posing Questions
4. Putting Ideas on the Table
5. Providing Data
6. Paying Attention to Self and Others
7. Presuming Positive Intentions

I encourage all PLC's to follow the norms of collaboration. As I plan meetings, I also use this structure so the process is seamless for all interactions that take place with stakeholders.

A great resource to use as a leader working with PLCs is Austin Buffum's and Mike Mattor's ***It's About Time***. This book gives ideas on how to implement interventions and extensions during the school day. Remember, urban environments must rely on school time to impact instruction. We now know, it is the school's responsibility to ensure the student's scholastic needs are met. We need to accept the children for where they are academically, work with them and not accept failure or excuses for students falling behind. In a perfect world, all educators would ensure that prevention is used instead of intervention. In urban settings with high transiency, you must rely on interventions to bring learners to their correct grade level but also offer above grade level learners the opportunity to grow. Teachers may feel they need additional professional learning to increase pedagogy. I noticed with increased professional learning, educators can become easily overwhelmed trying to implement everything they have learned. This causes the focus to be too wide and can lead to educator frustration. It is imperative that you use the data from the PLC's to create the professional learning opportunities that the majority of the staff feel is needed.

PRINCIPAL'S ROLE IN PLCS

As an administrator, it is imperative that you attend as many of the PLC meetings as possible. When you join in the meeting, make sure you are an active participant. Your contribution should be supporting staff, offering advice or resources to assist. This also gives you a good pulse of what motivates your staff and the barriers they face in implementing the school's mission and vision.

I gain great insight about my staff from attending these PLC meetings. I support the growth of educators by conducting learning walk-throughs and sharing my feedback with teachers. This helps me identify who the teacher leaders are in the group. I am also able to observe which teachers were working hard and implementing best practices in their instruction. **This practice is paramount to ensure that what you're hearing in the meetings is occurring in the classrooms during observations.**

Remember, you are the instructional leader of the school and when you attend PLCs, it is imperative that you are an active participant. There are many times I visit schools, and the principals might be physically present but not mentally present. They have their emails open and are not engaged with the topic of the PLC. Attend with an open mind, understand the pulse of the meeting and contribute.

Another critical task is to ensure that your School Improvement Team provides timely feedback to the PLC's. The School Improvement Team should observe and gauge that the PLCs are aligned correctly as well as ensuring they have the necessary resources to perform their tasks. *Alignment* is defined as, ensuring that teachers who share students or content areas have time to co-plan lessons and also write and design grade level assessments together. Feedback from the administrator helps the PLC grow; however, feedback from peers ensures there is cohesiveness amongst the staff. As a leader, you want to build the master schedule to allow common planning time. Depending on your district, you may or may not have funds for before or after school PLCs. If those are not options, you need to design the master schedule with that in mind. I discussed this in a previous section and gave you resources on how to create a detailed, learner-friendly schedule.

Feedback from the administrator helps the PLC grow; however, feedback from peers ensures there is cohesiveness amongst the staff!

SUMMARY OF COLLABORATE

Professional Learning Communities, or PLC's, have many different names and shapes depending on where you are located. The importance of the PLC's is to have educators converse with their peers about effect instruction. Well run PLC meetings focus on student data and student work samples. Once those are dissected, interventions are custom-built based upon what the data shows is deficient.

As a leader, it is imperative that you attend, are vested in the interventions, and ensure that the PLCs report to your School Improvement Teams what transpires in the meetings. Once data is provided, via a template, it is equally as important for the

Improvement Team to provide feedback to the PLC's. This flow of information ensures accountability while also allowing your School Improvement Team to understand what is taking place in these meetings.

As a School Improvement Team, these meeting minutes for the PLC's should be requested after each meeting and they should be discussed by the Improvement Team at least once per month. The data you collect will provide valuable insight into the Professional Learning that you need to provide to the PLC's. This is a great way of sharing information between all parties.

As this practice becomes engrained in your school culture, it will become paramount that you use these groupings to build your master schedule in forthcoming years. I also ensure that these meetings are not interrupted with topics that should be discussed via email or through a school staff meeting. The entire meeting and collaboration should be focused on student improvement and achievement.

The final role, as the leader of the building, is conduct walkthroughs with simple "look fors" so you can also substantiate what the PLC's are reporting to your school improvement team. This allows another validity point to demonstrate that practitioners are using the suggestions of the school leadership team and finding value in them.

When you focus on student achievement, you are able to move the needle toward student growth!

5 INTEGRATE
IDEAS TO KEEP THE MOMENTUM GOING

"School transformation is the outcome of individual transformation"
Steven Covey

HUNTER'S PRINCIPAL PHASES OF LEADERSHIP DESIGN PROCESS

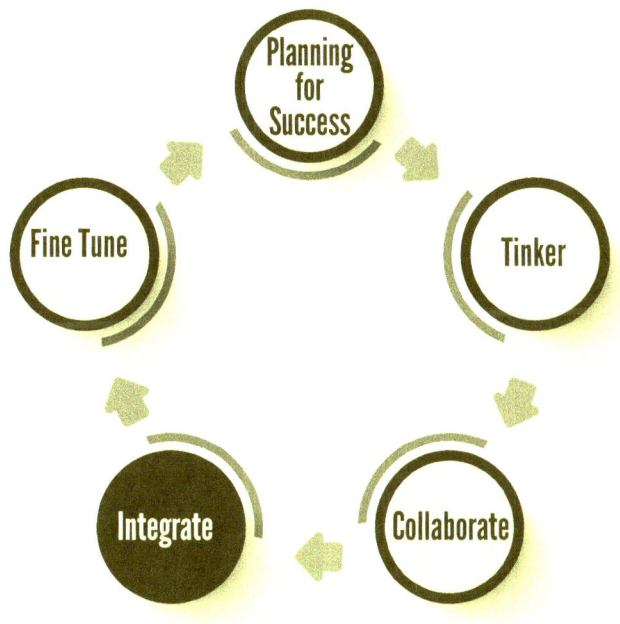

When you ask educators to make big changes, some will hide and not attempt it in fear of failure or some will work themselves into a burnout trying to make it happen. Pose this question to your staff; ask them, "If everyone increased their focus and effort 5%, what would change?" Just 5% more effort by everyone in your organization would solidify your role as a change agent.

Nathaniel Branden, who is considered the father of the self-esteem movement, created the 5 percent practice. He asked, "If I were 5 percent more responsible today, what would I be able to do?" This kind of thinking is what is needed as an urban leader. Give it a try! We know if you improve your scores in each subject area by 5%, a significant gain would occur at your school. John Maxwell states, "Success is gained in inches not miles." In this phase, it is imperative to disseminate the items you and your School Improvement Team collaborated on. This may seem like a daunting task. However, after meeting with your School Improvement Team, you should be able to find one academic and one social/emotional component to focus on for the next school year. You cannot ask your staff to change an initiative mid-year. You can fine-tune, but you cannot ask them to change their way of instruction to incorporate something new without sufficient training and practice. One way to reduce the learning curve of the change initiative is to provide the new content to your teacher leaders prior to implementation. This way, they can familiarize themselves with the new content. By doing so, when you present the information to the staff, it will show that everyone's voice was heard. Educator buy-in, which is so important to the implementation of any change initiative, becomes much easier when the majority of the staff sees the Improvement Team and the principal working together for the betterment of the staff and students. This demonstrates **Shared Leadership** and provides a voice for every stakeholder. I normally will ask teacher leaders to create talking points around the new initiative. Teacher leaders provide samples of how they would assess and implement the ideas in their classrooms and what the assessments would look like.

Having a unified, shared approach will decrease the implementation time and move you closer to reaching your goals. This process should take place anytime you are asking your educators to change the curriculum or strategies they use in their classroom.

SHARED LEADERSHIP

I gave a few ideas in a previous chapter about how and why Shared Leadership is beneficial to organizations. Coming from the business world, it amazed me how much time was spent on changes or issues that did not directly affect the school environment. Does it really matter where the paper is stored for the copy machines? Is this really the type of decision that an instructional leader should be making? In my opinion, these types of decisions distract from the mission of the school. Allow your Teacher Leaders to make these decisions. Allow them to query the staff and handle the things that are not instructional in nature. My second year in leadership, and every year thereafter, I have empowered my staff to make the decisions that inundate so many leaders. It freed me to assist in instruction. Many leaders I meet are so busy during the day making these minuscule decisions, and in return, they feel they are excellent managers. But in reality, they are tackling the decisions that do not impact instruction.

LASER FOCUSED ON STUDENT ACHIEVEMENT

I chose the words *to integrate* because throughout this book, I have integrated personal ideas and offered proven action items as an urban school leader along with the experiences of professionals in the industry. Now is the time to integrate all the items that were discussed, thus far, and guide your staff in being, "Laser Focused on Student Achievement." When I enter a classroom, the learners know I am in there for one reason only, to see the quality of instruction they are receiving. I visit each classroom multiple times throughout the day for a minimum of 35% of my day. The hours I am not able to get into the classrooms, I ask staff to place student work in my mailbox so I can do a quick review and stay abreast of the quality of assignments and lessons. Through mentoring of other administrators, I find they are overly focused on checking teachers' written lesson plans. I normally only spend about 5% of my time checking lesson plans, mainly just to grasp where the educators are in the curriculum.

I have found some educators can write excellent plans and not execute them at all. As a principal, the most crucial element is the delivery of content and the inquiry that takes place during instruction. I like to see guiding questions in plans, objectives and assessment/outcomes. By checking student work samples, you see how the educator is meeting the needs of his/her learners, if students truly understand the content and are completing the assignment. Another critical piece is to ensure when checking student work samples and lesson plans, you look for the integration of the new ideas. As a frontrunner, ensure the professional learning you have provided is being integrated. If you see non-evidence-based strategies being used in classrooms, you need to re-teach or model, in a non-confrontational way, successful strategies to the educator. Once again, make sure the conversation is safe and occurs in the classroom with a coaching tone of voice.

    One of the things I witnessed when first coming to my school and visiting classrooms was "Popcorn Reading." This has been found through numerous studies to be a <u>highly</u> <u>ineffective</u> way of teaching fluency & comprehension. I walk into classrooms and one student is reading from the textbook while the teacher corrects him/her when an error occurs. The other students in the class were in what I called a "boredom trance." They were compliant but not engaged and surely not working at their highest level. As I think to myself, there was probably not a bit of dopamine flowing in these students. Is this what is best for students? Many educators still feel that compliance over engagement is suitable for instruction. I was able to implement, with the support of the School Improvement Team, Guided Reading. There are numerous types of reading programs, and they all have pros/cons. We selected Guided Reading due to its ease of implementation. The truth of the matter is, any small group reading instruction lowers their level of frustration and increases the reader's confidence. Now that you are viewing student work samples and ensuring the ideas gained from professional learning are being implemented, you are ready to develop your staff. John Maxwell states that a leader should, "…give 80% of his/her effort to the top 20% of the most critical decisions." For principals and educators, this is very simple and straightforward. You should spend 80% of your energy on increasing student achievement. That leaves 20% of your effort for the other matters that do not impact student learning. Your assistant principal, if you have one, should be handling the items that take you away from the 80%.

As you integrate ideas into action, you will get disagreement from educators. It is essential your teacher leaders embrace the school vision that, *"If it's not best for students, it will not be discussed in a leadership meeting."*- Carol Dweck. She is the mastermind behind the Growth Mindset movement. Dweck also states, "...*most educators are content with teaching performance goals; however, we should be teaching learning goals."* Carol goes on to quantify and use the following example, "Getting a letter grade of "A" in French is a performance goal. Being able to speak French is a learning goal." We want all our students to be able to accomplish learning goals.

MAXIMIZING TIME FOR STUDENT ACHIEVEMENT

Here are a few excellent questions from the book

It's About Time by Mike Mattos and Austin Buffum:

1. Are we using our minutes wisely or taking extra minutes to line up students?
2. Are we picking up our students on time or wasting minutes arriving late?
3. When the bell rings at the beginning of the day, are our students in their seats ready to learn, or do we lose five to ten minutes moving about the room before taking attendance?
4. How soon do we finish teaching for the day, or do we utilize every possible minute we have allocated before packing up?

PARENTAL CONFERENCES

So how can we engage parents in their child's education? I often hear how parents are not involved in their child's learning experience. In educational circles, you hear the perception that parents don't care anymore. My experiences, on the other hand, produce different results. Parents do the best they can with the tools they have. If they had negative experiences in school or with teachers, it is hard for them to overcome these thoughts. I invoke a practice that is successful in an urban environment. I have a personal conference with every single parent in my school. I compile data and discuss the student's strengths and weaknesses on standardized tests. I give them a list of resources, websites and worksheets, and solutions to problems. I highly recommend planning these meetings into your schedule. Parents that generally may have an adverse view of the school have changed their demeanor entirely. They enjoy the sharing of data about their child. And better yet, you are getting valuable time to discuss how, as a community, to improve the school.

I cannot quantify if this improves test scores, but I ensure from research and personal experience, this leads to more academic conversations in the household. It gives parents insight into the classroom in a format that is different from the classroom teachers. Some parents don't feel comfortable talking to a teacher for fear of retaliation or other reasons. Parental conferences give time for an analytical approach, sharing of academic strengths and weaknesses, while behavior is not the primary focus of the meeting. Does this take a lot of time? Yes, it takes over a week to complete, and sometimes I meet with parents again throughout the year to see if growth has occurred. We must praise our parents who accept the challenge and need to include them in the successes of their child.

CONFERENCE STATEMENT EXAMPLE:

Dear Mr. or Mrs._____, I want to share the most recent assessment data with you. Your child, _____, is doing very well in <u>Reading Comprehension</u>. He/She scored above _____% of the other students, district wide. We are proud and will continue to assist him/her with improving. I want to mention an area or two where he/she is struggling. We have noticed after looking at this summative data and the teacher's formative assessments, that **math fluency** is a major issue for your child, _____. I want to know if you would be willing to assist us with practicing **flashcards for 5 minutes each night with your son or daughter. Here is a set of flashcards and some extra worksheets.** I know together we can continue to help _____ in order to fulfill goals set by him/her and by you.

Why is this meeting necessary? It is imperative to assist and model how you can slowly close the gap between urban families and the school system. This does so much for the entire district and helps with everything from passing levies to improving student behaviors. Also, as Daniel Pink states in his book *Drive*, "Rewarding an activity will get you more of it. Punishing an activity will get you less of it." Why did I choose this quote? I chose this specific quote to use as a reflection tool. How often do you or a staff member call or connect with parents only when students are in trouble? We run the risk of never connecting with parents of students who don't get in trouble. At my school, I created a straightforward Google form that encourages teachers to make positive phone calls each week.

THE FOLLOWING ARE GREAT STAFF MEETING QUESTIONS FOR PARENTAL INVOLVEMENT:

1. How can we create a more parent/guardian-centered school?

2. How can we inform our parents when their child does something positive? It must be more than a smiley face in a planner or merely writing "good day" in their journal.

3. What can the leadership of the school do to increase a positive culture during parental interactions?

4. How will having a more connected parental base assist with improved test scores?

HATTIE'S IMPACT ON STUDENT INSTRUCTION

John Hattie has researched and created meta-analysis for effective educational practices. The staff and I completed a book study on Hattie's work and attended professional learning on how we can implement the highest effect size practices into our daily instruction. We came to realize the effect size of a year of growth is .40. Since we now know the baseline, we began to look at what practices are currently used in our classroom. As we look at the topic of SOLE (described in the next chapter), we found that the evidence-based practice of having the students complete a JIGSAW Strategy about the topic, yielded a far greater gain than a gallery walk. This was just the beginning of using Hattie's research to empower our staff to work smarter and not harder. We wanted the students to be exhausted when they left school every day due to learning. In my first few years, though, the staff looked exhausted and my students looked rested. Hattie's research is mainstreamed now and the effect sizes can be adapted to the needs of your school. My one suggestion is not to incorporate all of the high effect size practices all at once. Be mindful of the time it takes to implement such change and the amount of professional learning that has to occur for the implementation to be successful.

IMPLEMENTING HATTIE'S EVIDENCE BASED STRATEGIES

As I mentor principals, I have suggested selecting one evidence-based practice with your School Improvement Team and using that specific strategy to drive improvement. It is best to see if there is already a trained educator in the district who would be willing to assist instructors and other staff members at your building with the selected evidence-based strategies and in-depth discussion.

"DON'T MISTAKE ROUTINE FOR COMMITMENT."

Educators have routines and can go through the motions without being committed to the learning goals or needs of the students. In other words, having set procedures and routines do little to drive student achievement. One example would be having students copy the definitions for vocabulary words out of the glossary. This has been proven through Marzano's Strategies' for Vocabulary Acquisition to be an inferior way of acquiring vocabulary knowledge. There is a process to have for vocabulary acquisition and transfer into the long-term memory. The above practice does not yield any lasting results. Another example of a misleading, underachieving routine is an educator completing a worksheet with the students. While the practice is important in most content areas, if the remainder of the students are just filling in the answers and not participating, it has little, if any, educational benefit. An acceptable practice, in contrast, would be for the students to complete the worksheet and the educator review any frequently missed questions. The benefit to the students is they are only receiving instruction on the questions that were problematic, instead of the teacher leading them through the assignment. **The educator may have exceptional classroom management but be unable to commit to trying the evidence-based practices that produce the highest student growth.**

GROWTH MINDSET AND FIXED MINDSET WITH INTRINSIC MOTIVATION

Having intrinsically motivated learners is genuinely the only way to improve student performance. Yes, you can get short-term gains with the "Stick" approach. The analogy, ***The Carrot and the Stick***, mentioned previously, is used a lot in the business world. The theory is you can dangle a "carrot", a reward, and some will reach for it, or you can threaten the workforce with a "stick", fear, to get them to your goal. The research shows that the latter is short lived. The same concept applies just as accurately towards education. You cannot scare someone into learning. You may be able to get a quick gain by threatening people or dominating over them, however, it will be short-lived, and it is not scalable. In the book ***Drive*** by Daniel Pink, an analogy is used comparing Microsoft Encarta and Wikipedia (mentioned earlier). Pink goes on to mention how very few people ever thought Wikipedia would outlast Encarta, that the billion-dollar behemoth, Microsoft, would lose to an open-source group of people who are motivated to share their knowledge. This is true, and Wikipedia is used and trusted throughout the world. It is an open source product, where anyone can add information and then it is vetted through a process. The people who support Wikipedia are intrinsically motivated to use the service and give back their expertise in the field. When someone purchased Encarta, he or she was motivated by trying to find information.

We need learners who are intrinsically motivated to meet the academic goals that we set forth for them. This is where the work of Carol Dweck really comes into focus. I have mentioned the **Growth and Fixed Mindset** and how it relates to education. She gave a fantastic example of a situation that occurs quite frequently in Urban America. A student is asked to complete an assignment, and he/she says, "I am not doing it." The instructor informed the student that he or she must call their parent or guardian and inform them, "Mother, in this school, we have to learn, and my teacher says I can't fool around, so, will you please come to pick me up?" This sounds so trivial, but you are showing the child that school is for them not for us as adults. Dweck goes on to further state, "When teachers are judging students; students will sabotage the teacher by not trying. But when students understand that school is for them, a way for them to grow their minds, they do not insist on sabotaging themselves." **Therefore, I place such a substantial academic focus on improving a student's mindfulness.** We can push curriculum and numerous academic initiatives, however, if the students are not able to learn, you are wasting valuable instructional time.

Why are schools a place where only students learn? Can't educators with a growth mindset learn at school also? This was a question that Dweck also posed in her book *Mindset*. She states, "Fixed mindset teachers often think of themselves as finished products." Their role, I feel, is to impart their knowledge. A good teacher is one that learns along with the students. Teaching the same curriculum year after year will make even the most focused educator stale, boring and complacent. What if we showed our students that we were vulnerable to learning and making mistakes, as well? What if we were the model for a growth mindset in our classroom? I like to think of extraordinary educators who are not interested in only teaching their students but who are interested in learning with them.

As a leader, I have used the following quote daily to keep myself focused, "**I never stop trying to be qualified for my job.**" This was written by Darwin Smith, the former CEO of Kimberly Clark Corporation. What if we took that initiative and applied it to the way our educators think? That is indeed a growth mindset and one that will yield tremendous results. Studies after studies have shown that people struggle with estimating their own abilities. If you take the mindset that you are continually learning as a leader, you will relish and become obsessed with the improvement of the whole organization. The rest of the staff will follow your lead, and the organization will soar.

Educators who have students with the fixed mindset can plan activities that assist the students with obtaining more Dopamine. Dopamine is a learning-friendly neurotransmitter associated with pleasurable feelings, motivation, memory, and focus. The analogy has been used so much that our society is addicted to Dopamine. Every time a cell phone beeps, a dopamine drop occurs. You are wondering who is texting or emailing you. Dopamine decreases anxiety in school and increases memory. To improve learners in our schools, we must use, as Dr. Judy Willis states, a "Dopamine Reward Cycle." Dr. Judy Willis is a renowned neurologist and former classroom teacher. I find it very important to understand brain function from a neurologist standpoint and figure out how we can improve the growth mindset and intrinsic motivation. Dr. Willis states, "Stress blocks the flow of information through the brain." The only correct way to combat stress is to have achievable challenges that students can complete. This does not mean easy work that is below grade level. On the contrary, it states explicitly, work that can be accomplished with structure will trigger a Dopamine Drop and a continual response to growth.

CHALLENGE FOR STAFF

1. What are some possible activities you can plan for your class today and tomorrow to promote growth mindset?

2. How, as the principal, can you have achievable goals for your staff to ensure Dopamine flows in their brain, as well?

3. Why is brain function essential to understand as an educator? How can you use the growth mindset to move learning into your classroom?

"NOT THE PROGRAMS IT'S THE PEOPLE"
Todd Whitaker

I visit other schools and speak with district leaders; they find excitement about new programs that will change their test scores. It's usually no surprise; unfortunately, I find out the next time we converse, they were unable to get staff buy-in. We are all duped into believing that the programs will improve and motivate our students. This is 100% inaccurate. The programs will not get the students to mastery; the educators will. Robert Marzano goes on to state that the following must be mastered for actual growth to occur:

1. Classroom Management
2. Academic Vocabulary
3. Academic Literacy
4. Learning Environment of School

These above mentioned strategies were taken from ***Classroom Instruction that Works***, by Robert Marzano. There are more strategies in his publication; however, I chose to focus on these.

If these four fundamentals are not followed, no program will be successful. If the above is done well, it will be because of exceptional educators. **So, once again, it's not the programs we buy, it's the educators we hire and develop.**

Summary of Integrate

This is the section where you initiate taking all the ancillary pieces and using them to improve the mission of your school. John Hattie's studies state, "...student's disposition to learn yields a .61 growth rate." An effect size of .4 is equivalent to one year's growth. In this section, we discussed multiple ways to increase your student's disposition toward education. This can be changed at the principal level by creating a climate that is conducive to learning and by integrating parents and community leaders into the process to further motivate and support the children you serve. I am a firm believer you place the most resources by your best people. The teachers who produce results and who are advocates for their students, parents, and stakeholders need to be provided with every possible resource for their mission. For instance, sending an educator who is not motivated to a professional learning opportunity may not be the best use of taxpayer funds. I will normally send one of my highest achieving educators and then ask them to share what they gained from the experience. If another educator inquiries about or asks for more information, I then look for opportunities for that educator to attend. **Always make your decisions with your best people in mind!**

The integrate section is one that you must re-read multiple times throughout your tenure as we can lose focus of how important all these items are to the success of the school.

6 FINE-TUNE
Professional Growth and Ongoing Change

"The Uncreative mind can spot wrong answers,
but it takes a creative mind to spot wrong questions"
John Maxwell

HUNTER'S PRINCIPAL PHASES OF LEADERSHIP DESIGN PROCESS

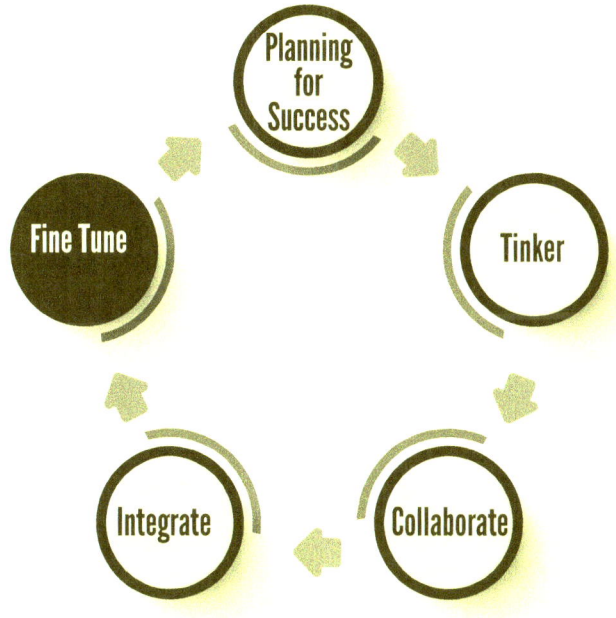

I spend a lot of time developing and honing in on my leadership skills through numerous publications on leadership. There is tremendous value in bettering yourself. If you advance the people around you, you advance the organization. It is crucial to have a School Improvement Team that has the same drive and commitment that you do to better the organization.

Start with Why by Simon Sinek

As you look to fine-tune your school, focus on growth opportunities that cultivate engagement instead of demanding compliance. Remember the quick story about the carrot and the stick? The "stick" demands compliance while the "carrot" helps with engagement. Simon Sinek's book *Start with Why,* mentioned above, fits perfectly into the **fine-tune paradigm**. If you are leading a school that does not know its own identity or loses track of its "why?" from time to time, it will be tough to sustain and scale growth in the organization. As educators, we are quick to say, "Here is how you solve this problem." As an alternative, we should be starting with, **"Here is why we are solving this problem. Now, let's work on solving it together."** In education, we tend to lower our expectations to ensure compliance that doesn't show lack of motivation. For example, I have witnessed in schools very weak rules and even weaker consequences. Please understand, I am not a big advocate of harsh and draw-the-line consequences.

As the prominent coach, John Wooden, would state, "Make every day your masterpiece." We must make every day count for our students and our stakeholders. As you begin to understand the priorities of all stakeholders in the process, invest the majority of your time to get the most significant return on your investment.

Here are questions I would like you to ask yourself. Spend some time alone, reflect and write down your responses to these questions:

1. What renews your energy?
2. What feeds your soul?
3. What gives you emotional strength?
4. What improves your mind?

HOW DOES YOUR ENERGY EBB AND FLOW?

These questions were taken from one of John Maxwell's books. It is as vital for us as leaders to remain grounded and self-reflective in our practice. That is the essence of this section.

Fine-tuning your school requires you to disseminate all of the summative and formative data you have at your fingertips. My first suggestion would be for you to create a chart with all the academic designations on your state's standardized tests. In my current state, terms include, Limited; Basic; Proficient; Accelerated and Advanced. After you have the chart created, list or have each teacher list their previous students' scores on the document. This is a great visual reminder of how effective our curriculum and instruction is for our learners. After you have that data documented, it is vital to update it the following year when you take quarterly assessments. There are numerous products that will correlate this data to your state designated tests. Some examples of the products are NWEA Map, STAR Assessments, and Terra Nova, to name a few. Once you have that data, you correlate what percentage of students will score proficient or higher on the End of Year exam. The data may not be 100% accurate as students are not fixed objects. However, it will allow you to fine-tune instruction, tutoring, and interventions.

Once you have the data from the first quarterly assessment, break the students' scores down into groups and discuss this data with your teachers. What are we going to do to move each child up at least one designation?

STAFF DEVELOPMENT QUESTIONS

1. As we look at the data, what is the one commonality that all the data has in common?
2. Did the teachers who used our evidence-based strategies produce substantial gains?
3. Did any of the tutoring help to move a learner up one designation?
4. What strategy can we start to implement to produce higher student gains?
5. Have each teacher look at the students from their classrooms, break down the data per student, and ask them to give you some feedback. This is crucial to self-assess and offer staff feedback.

ONGOING QUESTIONS

We discussed the first staff meeting previously, so we will delve into some topics that should be addressed prior to the next school year with your **School Improvement Team:**

1. What soft skills, i.e., empathy, perseverance, metacognition, will be focused on this year?
2. What will our positive discipline program look like?
3. What after-school programs were successful and yielded results?
4. What are our academic priorities this year?
5. What corporate sponsors do we currently have, and which ones can be grown organically or potentially started?
6. What parent groups are current and how can they integrate into the learning environment?
7. Why do PLCs matter and do they genuinely help student achievement?

*We will discuss each of the items above and mention a few others in this section.

Why are schools looking at teaching soft skills? Through current brain research and by working in urban schools, we need to find other ways to improve student learning. We know we only have our students for approximately 6 hours per day. As a staff, we study ***The Habits of the Mind*** and find metacognition defined as "Metacognition is, put simply, thinking about one's thinking. More precisely, it refers to the processes used to plan, monitor, and assess one's understanding and performance." John Hattie has proven through his meta-analysis studies that educators who use metacognitive strategies could yield an effect size of .53 growth or a half of a year's growth. There are numerous programs in the mainstream that can be utilized. Our school has used **Habits of the Mind**. We have narrowed the focus down to six topics per year, and then each year we add a topic or two. The previous year, we decided upon the following:

- Perseverance
- Striving for Accuracy
- Metacognition
- Managing Impulsivity
- Creating, Imagining, Innovating
- Listening with Understanding and Empathy

We have seen a moderate increase in student empathy and other habits we teach daily after adopting **Habits of the Mind**. We are able to determine that behavior has improved by teaching these strategies, and tracking every behavior infraction that happens in the school. We noticed that the teasing, bullying, arguing, and referrals decreased by 17% the first year we started to focus on listening with understanding and empathy. It is difficult, though, to quantify if these soft skills improved tests scores. However, we would argue that implementing these practices improves school climate which leads to more learning and fewer interruptions. If your school is anything like my current school, transiency is a significant problem. Our student roster looks totally different by the end of the year when compared to the roster from the beginning of the year due to student transiency, a 35% rate, in fact. That means that out of 100 students, only 65 will be in my building when the standardized tests are given. And of that 35%, the rate can increase to over 70% year to year. So, educationally, continuity is very hard to track. Nevertheless, we know that if we improve social skills, the learner will be able to be successful wherever they may continue their educational journey.

It is also paramount that you keep a pulse on your staff, i.e., morale, engagement, and overall health of the culture. Hattie states, "Teacher Self-Efficacy is the most significant factor in increasing scholastic achievement." You cannot have the mentality of us versus them (administration versus teachers). I see this repeatedly in public education. Make a point to your staff that your office is just an extension of the classroom. Whenever students are in your office, regardless of the reason, they should have an opportunity to learn. Teachers will, more than likely, be more supportive of you if you utilize your office to continue students' education. I have novels, short reads, math flash-cards and STEM types of activities in my office for the use of the students. They need to know that I am laser focused on student achievement. Have students read while they are in the school office waiting for you to finish paperwork, for example, or finish a call. We need to get out of all the punitive punishments that have ruled our educational systems.

You cannot penalize your students to proficiency!

ACADEMIC PROGRAMS THAT YIELD RESULTS

Here is a short list of programs that we have produced high academic results in my school:

- Math Counts
- Chess Club (.34 Effect Size)
- Science Olympiad
- Quiz Bowl
- Lego League
- Medical Club
- 24 Math Game Club
- Novel Club

These programs have assisted our learners with improving self-confidence, perseverance, and challenging them in a competitive way to improve their content in all areas. You will notice a trend with these clubs, they are all academic. According to Hattie, academic afterschool programs can yield up to a .40 effect size for students. To get participation in the urban area, you need to understand that you are competing against sports, video games, and child care. The program must be worthwhile, which is why I highly recommend having outside mentors participate, as well as, offering a snack for the learners. Some examples of outside mentors include, but not limited to, volunteer parents, business professionals as mentors and professional tutoring agencies. You would be amazed at how hard students will work for goldfish crackers and a juice box. Remember, we first need to meet their needs for food, safety, and shelter. Once they have basic needs met, they can let their guards down and begin to reach their potential. This is not a list of all the programs we offer, nor am I saying this will yield school changing results. However, it will raise the academic aptitude and allow your learners who participate to gain confidence, not to mention the relationships they will develop with their peers and the adults who monitor and instruct them. Another incredible idea is to investigate a medical club if one is available in your area. As we move toward college and career readiness across all grades, there will be many jobs in the medical fields. This club can provide the motivation and is appropriate for learners of all grades.

    We started our students off gradually, having our 3rd-8th graders participate in basic dissections on squid, crayfish, fish and other small animals. This captivated a few learners to want to delve into larger feats, such as a rat and pig, etc. What an awesomely rare experience for the students! This offers a more diverse learning experience for students and also serves as a great way to build for their future interests. As a leader, you may be faced with a few staff members who complain and state, "Well, I always do that experiment with my 10th graders." Your response is, "I know! Isn't it great that our younger students can do this experiment also? I am so happy that you can find more rigors to go into your experiment or other experiments to challenge the students." Do not let the staff members who do their "one" project each year dictate how your students are going to learn. They are usually the most vocal person in the grade and want to make sure everyone knows that he or she is going to "hatch chickens" again this year. It's as if it's expected the entire school stops when they do their one project. There should be no limit to the amount of opportunity for our students!

I also want to present to you one of the new practices we are introducing and having some excellent, yet early, evidence of student depth of content. We are studying the effect size of this practice. It's called SOLE.

SOLE
SELF-ORGANIZED LEARNING ENVIRONMENT

The term SOLE was coined and developed by Sugatra Mitra from India. It stands for Self-Organized Learning Environment. It is being developed and used throughout the world, including in the United States of America. My school has adapted some of Sugatra's practices and put a little variance on it. We pose open-ended questions which take time to create, but a database does exist. We then assign the questions to various groups of heterogeneously grouped learners in the classrooms. They are given 15-19 minutes to research the topic via the Internet, preferably, and then create a display or presentation. There are rubrics and other deliverables; however, the content and delivery are entirely up to the group. Each person in each group is required to present the material at least once to the other groups. When they all commence, we summarize and take the best points from each group. We can also use this with a gallery walk where each group does a presentation to the other groups. This was an example after looking into John Hattie's research; we thought we could find a more impactful strategy to share the important work done in the SOLE groups.

Some of the questions we have used are:
- How are logarithms used in the business world?
- How does a person's environment test their strength?

We are gaining valuable evidence and formulating our effect size comparative to other practices to measure the value of this type of instruction. I encourage you to do your own research.

You can hear Mr. Mitra on **TED.com**, and there are many worldwide sites to assist with starting this activity in your school.

HATTIE'S EFFECT SIZE FOR LEADERS

Another critical piece of shared leadership is to locate other leaders who have the same kind of like-minded leadership that you possess. It is essential for you to have a confidant who acts as a sounding board to discuss topics. I have found 1-2 leaders whom I know have the best interest of all students in their buildings.

After hearing Professor John Hattie speak in Chicago, he opened my eyes to the **effect size** of leaders. After researching the topic with his peers, he formulated two separate paths that leaders fit into:

TRANSFORMATIONAL LEADERSHIP YIELDS A .12 EFFECT SIZE

The qualities are:
1. Inspirational motivation
2. Individualized support
3. Sets direction, vision, high expectations
4. Instructional Support
5. Buffering staff from external demands
6. Fair and equitable staffing
7. Easily accessible
8. High degree of autonomy

INSTRUCTIONAL LEADERSHIP YIELDS A .42 EFFECT SIZE

The qualities are:
1. Classroom observations
2. Interpreting test scores with teachers
3. Focusing on instructional issues
4. Ensuring a coordinated instructional program
5. Highly visible
6. Communicating high academic standards
7. Ensuring classroom atmosphere is conducive to learning

The debate on the above two examples of leadership remains, can you be an Instructional Leader but not a Transformational Leader? I believe the answer is no. Hattie made the same statement in his presentation but did not confirm it with evidence. Nevertheless, I believe there is hope that excellent principals and aspiring principals can have an impact on the **effect size** of instruction in school. What is even more compelling is the amount of support we can provide to staff to implement the practices that we know yield the best results. I would highly recommend purchasing Hattie's publications. It will enable you to research what the effect sizes are of your current practices and which practices you can implement to improve your scores.

Through Hattie's research, the majority of educators fit into these above paradigms, however, Hattie also provides further research on exceptional practices with enormous effect sites.

These practices are worth their weight in gold according to Hattie:

1. Leaders who see their major role is to evaluate their own impact (Effect Size .91)

2. Leaders who get everyone in the school working together to know and evaluate their impact (Effect Size .91)

3. Leaders who are explicit with teachers and students about what success looks like (Effect Size .77)

PROFESSIONAL LEARNING

Professional Learning is critical to the development of educators. However, many times educators don't even bother to use the content they gain from attending professional learning. I classify educators attending professional learning as either:

1.) Learners 2.) Vacationers or 3.) Prisoners.

If you send Vacationers, they will attend a session or two but will use the time to "get away" from reality for a bit with a computer, a snack or creating the grocery list, for example. Prisoners will, for instance, reluctantly go but will have a bad attitude, not learn anything and will roll their eyes and relentlessly complain, "I already do this." These examples may either make you snicker or make you angry but I speak the truth from my experiences. The Learners, on the other hand, are the educators who are excited to improve their practice and the first ones to implement what they've learned. Learners also want to share the information with you and their peers. They are the teachers to send to professional learning and use the "teach the teacher model" with their peers. Most likely, these teachers are already your highest performing educators. As Todd Whitaker says, "Make all decisions with your best educators in mind." Learners choose which PD to attend, as they are the ones who will implement this new learning in their classrooms. They are also the educators who will model for other staff members.

I also have the educator who attends professional learning give a brief synopsis with materials to the staff at various staff meetings throughout the year. This creates accountability and provides further learning opportunities for the entire staff.

As a leader, it is imperative to stay updated with current pedagogy. I recommend memberships to National Organizations such as AMLE, NCTM, and NSTA. The monthly and quarterly articles sent out on behalf of these organizations will help keep you current with curriculum and technology trends. I have used many of the articles in said publications at the building level, and at leadership meetings. When the principal is acting as the lead learner, he/she should summarize the articles, providing current and applicable short reads for continual learning.

Making Decisions with the Best Teacher in Mind
by Todd Whitaker

As Todd Whitaker states, "Many times it's not the programs, it's the people." This was the quote I kept close to me throughout my first four years leading this school. In the business world, you did not have a lot of new programs. You had teams of researchers or goals of growing the company, which was very easy to scale. In education? Not even close. A new program for each content area is developed and always changing, promising substantial scholastic gains. There again, no program is going to instruct your students the way an excellent teacher will. Do not get duped into thinking a self-paced curriculum can make up for an inept teacher. You have two choices, to either help the staff member (ideal) or move toward removing them (long and arduous process). I am not against having an ineffective teacher removed and believe if safety issues are relevant, they need to be removed, quickly. However, part of what we need to do as educators is to improve the staff we have. There is not a magic tree where you can select a teacher. It is our responsibility to develop our teachers and give them the supports that are needed to be successful in our buildings.

HERE IS AN IDEA THAT'S BETTER THAN A RED BULL

Use your leadership intuition to decide when the right time is to conduct this activity:

Step 1: Pass out a blank postcard to each staff member.

Step 2: Have them write their name and address on the blank side.

Step 3: Have the educators answer the following questions on the other side of the notecard:

1. Why did you want to be a teacher?
2. Who was your favorite teacher and why?
3. What is your greatest strength as an educator?

After this activity is done, collect the notecards and place a stamp on them. When the time is right to inspire your staff, place them in the mail as a reminder that you care about them. This small act will inspire your staff and also focus them on their mission as an educator.

For example, I have a staff member whom I have sent to numerous professional developments, encouraged through evaluations, had staff members work on motivating techniques, and yet, she still hugs the Basal as she teaches. No matter how hard we push & encourage, her students never score any higher than below average. Is it fair to the students who are in her class? NO! We should not accept this. When a staff member who is refusing to attend professional development states comments such as, "It is the same stuff all the time, and I already do it," something has to change. This mindset is even more difficult to convince. When I am confronted with situations or people like this, I normally find another teacher in another school for mentoring. I ensure that the school has the same demographics and whose test scores are higher than the struggling teacher who believes he/she, "knows everything." After I have located the school and reach out to the principal, I ask if he/she would allow one of my staff members to observe one of his/her master teachers in the specific grade level. An effective strategy is to have low performing teachers observe master teachers. After the observation takes place, as an educational leader, I must convey to him/her that change has to happen and that it is possible. If improvement occurs, then the formal assistance can stop. If the educator still is reluctant to change, you need to put this instructor on an improvement plan. If he or she does not improve using the required goals, the School Improvement Team and principal need to look at recommending intervention for termination. I have found that most of the time when you begin that process, the staff member either improves or transfers to another school. It is essential not to allow the teacher to just stay in the safe haven they are in. You cannot move a school forward with below average instruction in any grade. **Make the decisions with the best teachers in mind!** If you have a good idea, ask your best practitioners their opinion. They will respect you enough and will give you an honest opinion on the change initiative. This theory was also noted in Todd Whitaker's book ***What Great Teachers Do Differently.***

CORPORATE SPONSORS

This section is a crucial, non-scholastic item you must accomplish. With the lack of funds but endless needs of learners, it is paramount that you find companies that have a focus on volunteerism and multiple financial partners. Where I am located, there are only four substantial businesses, not including liquor stores or convenience stores, at that time. I made a close relationship with the factories that are in close proximity.

When I first arrived at my school, there was a fragmented relationship with a Fortune 500 company. The relationship was strained and barely hanging on, however, I knew that if I could reinvigorate the base, I could have a dominant partner.

This was like being handed a piece of unpolished silver. I knew that if I took time to polish the "silver", it would be a precious resource. My school had a few dedicated volunteers from this company willing to assist me with growing the relationship. I began to state my vision to the committed volunteers and asked what we needed to do to grow the relationship organically. **I truly had a mission to ensure every child had an advocate at the school!** The volunteers were focused on recruiting their peers. As a result, I created a presentation because I wanted to show the company how impactful their volunteerism could be. I made the production focus around the benefit their contribution would make, not only to their organization but also to the children at Chase STEM Academy. After the presentation, 25 new volunteers signed on to mentor and tutor students. Thus, began the change of one of the most important corporate relationships. In case you wondered how impactful that presentation was, the school received two $10,000 monetary donations and the company also sponsors all of our Lego League Teams, Girls on The Run and Back to School supply drives. I can't tell you what a relief it is to have that kind of financial support! This relationship has since evolved into a partnership. We have over 30 volunteers who come weekly to mentor students. I also reached out to numerous other factories and churches in the area. Here are a few items to ponder as you begin to establish and create partnerships:

1. Visit churches and religious centers that are located within your school's footprint. Make a point to meet with the pastor and share your vision for helping the community and ask what he/she thinks the biggest needs are. This action item is paramount if you wish to grow the community volunteer base and understand the representation of the community you serve.

2. Visit all companies within the contiguous area and introduce yourself. Explain your vision for the school and how their contribution can benefit the students. It is also a good idea to bring a student or two with you. Make sure you have parental permission first. Leave information and "swag" about your school. Follow up with a handwritten letter within five days thanking them for their time.

3. Ask your staff if they know retired teachers, parents or grandparents who would like to volunteer at the school.

4. Look for grandparent organizations. Grandparents or seniors are very reliable and can play a significant role in the schools.

Important Note: Make sure you have every volunteer who encounters students pass a background check. Your district should have a policy for volunteers. If a volunteer shows up prior to having this check completed, do not dismiss them. Until the correct approvals have been received, ensure they are always accompanied by a school employee.

I recommend you **do not** call nearby businesses and try to gain donations or support that way. After I receive parental permission, I bring some students along with me to the businesses. The result is usually very powerful. Once the donors see the actual students, of whom a donation helps, it personalizes the relationship. Also, do some networking with Rotary groups, as well, and find out what each member of the Rotary Group is passionate about. We have found some passionate business owners who are avid basketball fans; they now sponsor our school basketball team. In addition, we have found business owners who love medicine that have assisted us with medical clubs.

Once you have created the mentorship program, you must make sure the mentors are supported. Here are a few items we did to ensure hospitality was relayed to the mentors:

1. Created name tags for each mentor on a lanyard
2. A place for their personal belongings
3. Warm greeting from the secretary
4. Item or items to work on to add value to your learners
5. Contact information for yourself and teachers in the event there are issues
6. A survey at the end of each quarter
7. A message service for mentors in case of weather delays, etc.
8. Ensure they have passed all district background checks prior to working with students.

PARENT LEADERSHIP

There are specific books written on how to recruit and empower parents into the school improvement process. I am a huge advocate for including parents in change processes. My statement to you is that getting the right parents is more important than just getting parents who are willing to volunteer. I made the mistake of being so happy to get parents that I did not vet them enough to make sure they were the right fit. Some would walk into classrooms while instruction was taking place thinking they were helping, however, it caused some angst for the staff.

When you do find excellent parental volunteers, treat them as an essential component of the school. The vetted volunteers have relationships with parents in the community who promote the wonderful learning taking place inside your school. They also know the students from outside the school and may have interacted with them in the neighborhood. It's easy for a parent from the community to talk to another parent from the community. Don't try to relate to the problems or situations of your parents, allow people with authentic experiences to communicate with them. This doesn't mean you are hands-off, it means you stick to your expert area, which is instruction.

PARENT GROUPS AND FUNDRAISING

Having a PTO is a great start to achieving school community. But did you also know that there are some other excellent programs? How about father organizations such as The Watchdogs? I have tried various parents' organizations through the years, such as booster clubs, PTO's, parent-created. Some of them failed at times, yet been successful other years. With a transient school, it is vital that you keep recruiting and educating the parents you have. I have spoken with local unemployment agencies and Government Assistance offices and have found some parent volunteers who need to do volunteer hours to keep their benefits. This can be a great way to bring parents to school and have them help with office tasks, for example. Please keep in focus that you are not better than anyone. You need to accept parents for being the parent of a child in your school. I never look at a parent as someone less intelligent than me. I look at them as a person who is doing the very best they can for their child. If they need education, help them get the education. Bring a GED program to your school to assist with parents who do not have transportation. Find a way to include them in career readiness programs and allow them to sit in on classes to learn skills. When you include the community in the school, everyone prospers and improves. You get more help with honey than with vinegar.

These parents will also be needed for fundraisers at your school. A lot of monies will be coming and going and I choose to handle all the funds from fundraisers. I find it easier to ensure all the monies are allocated and accounted for. I mentioned this earlier in another section, and it is imperative to adhere to this. All items need to be accounted for and tracked as it is all related to public funds. Keep in mind that most fundraising companies will push their agenda and, be assured; you will be inundated with every type of fundraiser to sell.

Note-to-Self: If your school and the school families live in an impoverished community, you need to be aware that asking parents with little disposable income is problematic.

I have found that doing small things like a popcorn sale for $.50 is very beneficial with little pushback. Evaluating items and their cost is very important to ensure you sell adequate items and generate a profit for the fundraiser. I chose to allow all students the opportunity to participate and not just students whose parents have more disposable income. I also utilized our gym and have "open gyms" where the students and their parents can play basketball after school for $1.00. There are numerous companies that will promise enormous rewards for conducting their fundraisers. Be very skeptical of these in an urban environment as we have tried some of the fundraising programs and struggled just to break even. Healthy foods, dances, and parent versus student experiences are the items that urban parents place a priority on and have always supported at my school.

ASSEMBLIES

There are numerous companies who will vie for your Title One Funds or other monies. They will have sales pitches on how their programs will bring parents in or help with bullying. I have vetted numerous programs and have found a few that have proven to be exceptional in service and performance:

1. Bright Star Theater: Excellent for Black History Month and other specific performances.
2. Matt Wilhelm: BMX X –Game athlete with good anti-bullying story.
3. Mr. Peace: Great story about acceptance
4. Rainforest Live: Science Programs

Another beneficial assembly is to bring in an illustrator or author who fit the demographics of your school. This program is a great way to jumpstart any writing initiative. I have not contracted portable movie companies as the cost is prohibitive and the impact was not as prevalent as other assemblies.

POSITIVE DISCIPLINE

This term is loosely coined through the educational spectrum. There are numerous frameworks that are adopted each year, such as, *Restorative Justice*, PBIS, PBS, *Love and Logic, Adaptive Schools*, and multiple others. We use the PBIS framework along with **The Habits of the Mind** as a program to help students and teachers intelligently. When he or she doesn't know the answer, we can teach that child, or teacher, how to grow as a learner by following the guidelines of the program. There are numerous programs similar to **The Habits of the Mind**; however, our staff preferred the above due to the straightforwardness and attention to skills our students lack.

The most important thing is that you establish the non-negotiables at your school, meaning, behaviors that are never tolerated. Here are a few examples of non-negotiables for teachers:

1. Do not scream at students
2. Be positive when speaking with students from your classroom and other classrooms. This does not mean if you notice something that affects safety you look the other way.
3. Don't be angry if another teacher has a better relationship with one of your students.

Can you figure out why I listed these few non-negotiables? To better explain, this is what my staff would hear from me: "Students work for whom they respect. It's important to remember you are not one of them (a student), you are their instructor and they work for you when they can trust you." Remember, urban students have experiences that most of us have never had in our lives. Our role is not to feel sorry for the students. Our role is to push them in their educational journey by showing them perseverance, patience, honesty, respect, and trust. This can yield the results that didn't seem possible.

We held assemblies frequently to review the positive behavior expectations we expected and what was not allowed. My administrative staff came to an agreement that unless it was a major infraction, we would instruct the child what is expected. ***We need to educate urban students the same way we educate other students, and that's through rigor and accountability!***

As I mentioned above, there are numerous frameworks which I believe all have important components. I recommend studying all of them and, if needed, pick and choose which pieces of the framework are applicable to your school environment. As an example, we found that pieces of *Restorative Justice* work very well with our students. We agree that being "restorative" is the correct way to use positive discipline. In the book **Better than Carrots or Sticks**, the author gives some tremendous impromptu questions for teachers to ask their students in private settings:

1. How do you describe yourself?
2. How do other people describe you?
3. What assumptions do teachers make about you that are not true?
4. How would you like others to describe you?
5. Let's plan to get you where you want to be. Shall we begin?

These types of questions provide an additional tool for both educators and educational leaders to model for their staff. Another strategy I use from the above-mentioned book that works well, is to conduct a classroom discussion using the following questions to guide the talk:

This is an excellent Brainstorming activity to discuss problem behaviors:

1. What is the problem our class is having?
2. Why is this a problem?
3. How does the problem make you feel?
4. What can we do about the problem? Let's brainstorm solutions.
5. What is our best solution?

I have used this activity when students have become disrespectful to a new teacher. It happens when, for instance, a teacher retires, becomes ill, or transfers to a different school. These strategies assist the new teacher with his or her classroom expectations as well as quell any angst the students feel about the change.

TEACHER VACANCIES

Let's discuss what happens when you lack qualified teachers in your school or have many long-term substitute teachers. This is something that will continue to be an issue if you teach in an urban environment. The statistics show that over half of all educators in urban environments leave the profession within five years. This does not have to happen at your school. At my current school, this has been the opposite. I have educators who've left and then later returned due to the transformation of the building. When the reputation of a successful school leader is discussed by teachers, you will find there are teachers who want to come and work with you. So, what do you do with long-term substitutes? Every year, since I have been an urban leader, we have had a shortage of Special Education teachers in my building. Having three units of severely behavioral, handicapped children, staffing is a continual problem. Administrators ask me what a leader can do to help retain licensed educators and assist the unlicensed with getting the correct licensure? The simple answer is **SUPPORT**. Support looks differently for these educators as they are in flight or flee battle each day with their students. When the students come in every day with a trauma level of 5 or higher, instruction cannot take place until their level is below a 2. To assist, I have solicited a mental health agency to place caseworkers in my building to assist children who have immediate needs. Of course, this takes parental consent. However, I have only met one parent out of over 100 that said "no" to the assistance. Now, this isn't a solution, but it allows the affected child to receive one-on-one attention and therapy services. This may not permanently fix the problem, and sometimes we must go through the same routine every day, but it does allow the educator to assist the learners who are on task and to improve their educational levels. Without finding licensed people to help your special education students, it is difficult to raise the scores of the subgroups. When you have a passionate individual, who is choosing special education as a second career, you have an opportunity to develop their skills all on your own. Each state has specific <u>emergency licenses</u> for educators. Once you know the person is committed, help them look for college programs that allow individuals with a bachelor's degree to obtain a Master's in Education in 1-2 years. It is vital that you help the person navigate this process. Don't just tell him or her about these programs; reach out to that person, and build a relationship with the university, as well. University Student Services can answer any question to quell any angst the person may have about continuing with the program. We owe it to all individuals, interested in education, to help further our mission. We never have enough passionate educators in the educational field, and we cannot rely on government entities to grow our profession. We must take the initiative and show how lives can be changed by having educated, caring people in our urban schools.

    When, regrettably, you have a long-term substitute teacher, who is not meeting the goals of the district or the school, it is essential to follow the district procedure for removal. While it is nice to have a teacher who comes every day, it is harmful to have the wrong one. This happened to me one year. As a principal, I was happy to have a teacher after weeks of daily substitute teachers, but

I became complacent. I was content when students were not being removed from class; however, I lost sight of what my mission was to all students. The students in that class did not deserve a complacent teacher or leader. I learned my lesson quickly as tests scores in those grade levels dropped significantly. The entire ordeal made me realize it would be better for me to teach the class than let a substandard educator hold my learners' education in his/her hands. Daily, I review students' scores on quizzes and formative assessments to keep abreast of how our students are performing. I will pull a few students down to my office each day or to the cafeteria to work on a standard they are struggling with from the previous year.

DAILY SUBSTITUTES OR NO CLASS COVERAGE

I make a point each day to announce on the morning announcements that we have a guest teacher in the building. This may seem like a trivial issue, however, I want to ensure the guest teacher feels connected to the school. It also shows support to provide them with my office extension number should they need to call for assistance. In addition, I visit this classroom a minimum of 4 times each day. When time permits, I will even take my work into the room to quasi-evaluate the substitute and the students. With the lack of substitutes in the workforce, you either take care of your guest teacher, or you have to find someone to cover the teacher's class. While sometimes having someone cover the class is easier with less effort from the administration, it is not what is best for students.

What about when there is NO substitute available to cover a class? Sometimes, another teacher may agree to be the substitute teacher and then combine the classes or split them up between classes. But even though students know and may comply with the rules of a full-time teacher, it is nearly impossible for even the best of educators to instruct a classroom full of a combined 45 students. The reality is the teacher's regularly scheduled classes suffer as the effort is made to build quick rapport with the other class.

Ensuring the absent teacher leaves complete lesson plans falls on the administrator. Having worksheet packets of meaningless work is not the solution to having a classroom full of compliant students. We only have 180 days of instruction and every day needs to be productive. Enforce that the teachers in your building leave grade-level review work or assignments that are challenging for students but not new material for the substitute to teach. Having a review day with math/ELA and other topics is a great way to gather data to see what the students have indeed learned. As the instructional leader, I also keep a "stash" of lesson plans in case the teacher was not able to leave plans. This usually takes care of any issues. However, when the absence lasts longer than one day, be prepared to assist in creating lessons. This situation is familiar to me as sometimes my full-time teachers may already have another class, and/or there just isn't an available substitute teacher that day. In this case, you have an option,
either you decide to teach the class yourself, or ask another educator to assist, as the students learning is your responsibility. Here's the summary, when you have educators who are absent and

no substitutes are available, depending on your district, you have a few options:

1. Cover the class yourself
2. Ask another teacher to cover the class
3. Split up the class

As you look at your options, none of these are ideal. Remember, it is not the student's fault there is a shortage of substitute teachers. Unless you are fortunate enough to have a full-time building sub., you are in the same boat as every urban school in America. I have used all three options and have had success with each. One piece of advice is to never, unless it's absolutely necessary, have the students move to another classroom unless it is one grade above or below their current grade. It is not recommended, for instance, to have 4th-grade students interact with an 8th-grade class. It creates too many potential problems, the language used in classes may or may not be developmentally appropriate, and the students can become frustrated. Also, ensure that if you do not have a teacher with strong discipline, do not put students in their classroom. Why? Because you would be better off teaching them yourself as they will probably be removed anyway, for behavioral issues. I had the foresight to prearrange a hybrid plan for a situation such as this where I instruct the class in the morning, in order to complete math and ELA, and then split the students in the afternoon.

BREAK THE NORM OF URBAN CHILDREN

A goal, we, as administrators, should strive to achieve is to break the stereotypes of urban children. A few statements for your staff to consider and discuss:

1. Everyone has a story, and no one is unique. No person has a better story than anyone else, they just may tell it better. Respect all students and staff members as you don't know what part of their story was written today.

2. Can you remember anything that your previous teachers have taught you? If not ask yourself why?

3. If a student's parent is incarcerated, so is the entire family. Please read that again. The trauma that the student feels is also felt by all siblings and other relatives.

4. You are the thermostat in your classroom, not the thermometer. Do not allow your students to raise the temperature. You control the temperature, and sometimes you need to turn up the heat.

5. We are not training our students to be parrots.

6. FAIL: First Attempt In Learning

Your staff is focused on student achievement and they are turning up the heat in their classroom. The following questions need to be cultivated to ensure all students are successful. We have encouraged the staff, and now we need to ensure we have the support for them to continue to be successful. Your educators should continue to ask themselves these questions while planning and meeting in PLCs:

1. What do we want the children to learn today?
2. How are we going to measure the learning?
3. What will we do with students that are Tier 3?
4. What will we do with students who are advanced?

Once educators use these questions as a framework in their PLCs, you know they are looking at ways for the students to be successful.

STAY INSPIRED

Constantly as a leader, I spend time visiting productive schools to learn what practices make them effective schools. One of the schools I visited with my School Improvement Team was featured on Oprah. Our group made the journey to The Ron Clark Academy and instantly envisioned the kind of student engagement that we needed at our school. We were mesmerized.

After meeting Ron Clark and spending two days at his fantastic school in Atlanta, GA, I gleaned many things I could implement at my current school. One of his quotes really resonated with me, "You can choose to spend your time at school however you choose, but you can only spend it once." This is a great mantra for staff and students to be aware of. If, as a leader of the building, you use every minute you are in the building to focus on student achievement, you will notice the entire culture of your school change. Mr. Clark has used the analogy, "…getting everyone on the bus," as to moving in the right direction. You will not be able to get everyone to be the "runners". However, you owe it to your "runners", and other high achieving educators, to ensure that your time and the time of your School Improvement Team demonstrates the right way to use time. Mr. Clark defines "runners" as the teachers who are continually moving the bus in the right direction. They run for new initiatives and are the ones that can single-handedly move initiatives and student achievement forward. It is very easy to get excited about an initiative, just remember that starting is the easy part. It's keeping the stakeholders engaged and continually monitoring the progress of the initiative that can be a test. Once you monitor the progress, share the results with the ones who are doing the work. It will either validate their hard work or allow them to critique and change what isn't working.

Here is a question your School Improvement Team needs to ponder: Think about your student's typical school day. How much of the day did they spend doing your work and how much of the day did they spend doing their work? We must ensure that lesson design is well thought out to create mastery experiences as well as continual engagement. Dr. Judy Willis, a renowned neurologist, and current educator states, "When students are joyfully engaged, their brains are able to process learning and store in long-range memory more efficiently. It is also important to impress upon your staff if you sit students down hour after hour, doing poor work, don't be surprised if they start to fidget." It seems so simple, yet we start out the year with engaging lessons and at the first sign of student conflict, we allow educators to slip back into their previous practice. In other words, if this occurs, *we don't have adequate support for teachers to take risks and sustain the risks.* If, as a leader, you are focused on achievement, you will offer ways to ensure that the students are actively engaged.

GROWING PAINS

These items may not become prevalent your first year. However, if you follow the framework I have provided, you may find yourself dealing with some of these items as I did. We had an increase of learners back to our school due to the improvement of the culture and test results. We had to move Art, Music and every other special program that previously had a classroom onto a cart. This is a tough decision for any principal at any stage in their career. We never want to devalue the specialists. However, we needed to ensure that the core class teachers were provided with the space they needed to educate. Notifying specialists of information as soon as you are notified goes a long way in the qualities of respect and trust for administration. You do not want to wait for your human resource department to let your staff know a change is coming. This is one of the issues we had with scaling the educational experience of our learners; we were out of space now. When I first arrived, we had six empty classrooms in the building; specialists utilized three of them. All six rooms are now occupied by our learners in content areas. We also drastically dropped our suspension rate by 500% and have sustained that level for the last five years. With the reduction of suspensions, educators now complete interventions in the classroom along with instructing all learners versus having students removed for chewing gum or being out of dress code, for example. In years past, students had to sit in the office when they were out of dress code or when parents were called for a change of clothing. We have created a system now where students can borrow a shirt or pants from the office and return to class immediately. As a group, we made this part of our operating rules. In the morning, in all classroom environments, math and reading are taught, and we cannot have students missing time due to things outside of their control. We spend time trying to find other resources for the children who are in need. This includes calling non-profits, local and state government entities and neighborhood churches for assistance. This is a function of the principal to ensure these relationships exist and the needs of the students are met.

We, as a school, will always have room for improvement as the transient rate of learners in urban areas is increasing and not decreasing. I had to increase the number of educators at my school due to an enrollment increase of 130 students in four years. My building, unfortunately, was not designed for this increase in student enrollment. As a leader, I had to ensure the culture of the school was accepting of new teachers and students, so they could step right in and feel welcome without any issues. This was very important as 80% of the staff had bought into both the culture and student-centered atmosphere, which everyone emulated each day. This did not happen in my first year as a leader, each year the percentage of staff buy-in increased. By the end of year two more than 80% of the staff was actively engaged. The challenge of my School Improvement Team was to ensure new staff member's become part of the 80 % and understood the vision of the school. Using a term from my business days, *scaling*, it was important for me to see the difference between scaling a business and scaling an educational organization. There was a huge difference between buying a few more assets in business to increase the bottom line and grow versus adding learners of all educational levels and attempting to keep the product the same. I knew at some point, I would take a small step backward, or under the best-case scenario, move only a small step forward. As I mentioned above, we increased the school from 220 students to 350 students during the first four years of my tenure.

Final School Improvement Meeting

Leadership Activity for School Improvement Team

When the School Improvement Team meets prior to the next school year, I recommend conducting a Keep/Start/Stop Chart:

Step 1: Create an anchor chart
Step 2: Label the chart, "What Should We?"
Step 3: Answer the following questions:

1. As a school, what should we **KEEP** doing 100%? Make sure it is research and evidence-based. Ex. Guided Reading, Reciprocal teaching

2. What new practice should we **START** doing? Will we need professional development?

3. What should we **STOP** doing and why?

- I encourage you to have staff work with an elbow partner and give them around 5-7 minutes to brainstorm.

- Once the anchor chart is completed, make sure you create a digital copy for your records to revisit it at a later staff meeting.

- Encourage staff to collaborate in the change process. *Now is a perfect time to solicit assistance from people who may not have volunteered, prior.*

Provide Post-It notes in order for educators to write down their opinions on the three topics:
- Keep
- Start
- Stop

Once this activity is completed, spend some time going over the above items, as a group, and brainstorming ways to implement practices or curtail any conflicts. We base this on the 80/20 rule. If 80% of the staff believes the idea is right, then we move forward. If less than 80% of the staff concurs, we table the discussion until we have the majority of buy-in from all staff. This is when it is important for your teacher leaders in their PLC's to have time to discuss the Keep, Start, Stop items and ensure the 80% goal is met.

Closing of the Building at Year's End

Well, you made it to the end of year one. Here are some items that your district may have you complete. Please, however, check with your district for the proper closing procedures already in place.

1. Hold an exit meeting. This is when you and your teacher leaders meet with each teacher to discuss next year's goals and reflect upon the past year.

2. Review the goals for the year with the School Improvement Team. Brainstorm how the team succeeded and needed areas of improvement. This is important to do as comments and questions are still fresh in their mind but will be forgotten over the summer.
3. Ensure any teachers who are transferring leave all the material in their classroom. Do not let a teacher leave the building unless they have checked out with you or your assistant. This is not a trust factor, this is a policy.
4. Make sure every educator leaves a copy of their grade book in their mailbox. In case a parent wants to contest a grade and the teacher cannot be reached over the summer, the gradebook is right at hand.
5. Make sure supplies are ordered to ensure a smooth opening of the next year. This is redundant because it's been mentioned in other chapters, however, it is vital.
6. Make sure you save all tardy slips, parent excuse notes, and other discipline documents. Your Board of Education should have a policy for how long to hold onto them before recycling. I have had to go back and look for excused absence slips from two years back.

Summary of Fine-Tune

It is necessary to understand that the **Fine-Tune** section is meant to make subtle changes. You need to make changes based on what the data is telling you. Every decision you make needs to be based on the evidence of what the data portrays. When people multitask, it is said that they can lose up to 40% efficiency on all topics. This is important that you focus on one thing at a time and not attempt to overtake all the deficient areas at once. If I could suggest one school change initiative to begin, it would be to focus on the improvement of student's writing, specifically, Claim-Based Evidence Writing. This is a Common Core and State Standard that every educator I spoke with has continually said their students struggle with.

As a leader, it is time to continually attend professional learning, and work on the leadership strategies that can improve your school. It's a great time to review *School Leadership that Works* by Robert Marzano for some evidence-based practices that yield gains. In Marzano's work, you will find practices that you, as a leader, partake in to improve the aptitude of students.

School Improvement Teams take many shapes depending on where your school is located. However, one thing is certain, you are the leaders of the building. You need to model effective practice and continually improve your leadership skills. Using Hattie's research should always be at the forefront of decisions you make. With the amount of meta-analysis he has researched, when you incorporate one of his strategies, you can be assured it has been proven effective if implemented well. This takes the focus off trying to find the strategies, trying to find the correct strategy for the issue and then assisting with implementation. You, in essence, can help with implementation, instead of trying to conduct research on what works.

Each year revisit what leadership practices have the greatest effect sizes. Starting your yearly planning with that data keeps everything in focus.

When I began to look at other ways to improve student achievement and focus on assisting the whole child, I kept bringing myself back to looking into the social emotional wellbeing of my students. I researched numerous frameworks and programs and settled on **The Habits of The Mind**. Once I had a thorough understanding of it, I pitched my idea to the School Improvement Team. We decided that implementing all the "Habits" at once was too much for the learners. We settled on a smaller number and were intentional on how they were instructed. I would recite information about them on the morning announcements. We stuck with one habit for each month and circled back to the same one after 6 months. This kept them in the forefront of students' minds.

When you look to add after school programs, make sure you have the support of staff or volunteers. It is very easy to become overwhelmed with ambitions to do everything and then quickly find your volunteers wane. I would suggest trying to implement clubs, after school, and find educators who are passionate about the content so; it is not more "work" for them and more about sharing their passion.

Sports are also a major item in urban environments, and basketball is, by far, the cheapest with the least amount of equipment. Start small and try to engage community groups to support your teams.

"The right word may be effective, but no word was ever as effective as a rightly timed pause," Mark Twain. I chose this quote as it emulates what your thought process should be your first few years. ***Remember Listen Before you speak!***

7 SUMMARY

> "IF A MOVEMENT IS TO HAVE AN IMPACT IT MUST BELONG TO THOSE WHO JOIN IT NOT JUST TO THOSE WHO LEAD IT"
> **SIMON SINEK**

In Daniel Pink's book, he retells the story of Microsoft Encarta and Wikipedia. If you had asked to predict the future, on which one would have been more successful, I guarantee the majority would have chosen Microsoft Encarta. However, we all know that Wikipedia is a site that is used millions of times a year. Why did it work? Wikipedia created a culture of others sharing knowledge for the betterment of society. Pink also goes on to state, **"Control leads to compliance; autonomy leads to engagement."**

As an educator with a background in high-level, senior management, it was paramount for me to put research into action. Theory and research are wonderful at the collegiate level of instruction, but if they are not broken down and disseminated to the practitioners; the theories will always remain theories in academia. This book will serve as a yearly guide for all new, seasoned, and aspiring principals. These ideas, thoughts, and evidence should be revisited monthly to focus on our most significant challenge, which is to continue to engage our students in worthwhile learning. As I continue to build the efficacy of my current school and research new ways to maximize student learning, I also use this framework as a reference to keep me focused on what I can do to help an organization operate at its fullest potential.

I will leave you with the story of Warwick, the Horse:

A man was lost while driving through the country. As he tried to reach for the map, he accidentally drove off the road into a ditch. Though he wasn't injured, his car was stuck deep in the mud. So, the man walked to a nearby farm to ask for help. "Warwick can get you out of that ditch," said the farmer, pointing to an old mule standing in a field. The man looked at the decrepit old mule and looked at the farmer who just stood there repeating, "Yep, old Warwick can do the job." The man figured he had nothing to lose. The two men and the mule made their way back to the ditch. The farmer hitched the mule to the car. With a snap of the reins, he shouted, "Pull, Fred! Pull, Jack! Pull, Ted! Pull Warwick!" And the mule pulled that car right out of the ditch. The man was amazed. He thanked the farmer, patted the mule, and asked, "Why did you call all of those names before you called Warwick?" The farmer grinned and said, "Old Warwick is just about blind. If he believes he's part of a team, he doesn't mind pulling."

This story emulates why it is so important to be part of a team. Your role is to serve the teachers, students, and stakeholders and have them follow you to the end goal. You have chosen this field to make a difference in the lives of students. You must continually improve and raise the standard of growth for everyone in the organization. DO NOT STOP once growth has occurred. ***Does Growth Ever Stop?*** You have the ability to change entire communities if you follow these paths and believe in yourself, your students and your teachers. ***Make it happen!*** Good luck!

OVER MY FIRST FEW YEARS, I HAVE BEEN FEATURED IN:

- Featured in the Toledo Blade for reducing suspensions from over 400 days to fewer than 60 days in one year.
- Leading my school to an energy conservation competition victory where we reduced consumption by 13%.
- Principal of the Year
- Over five-district video segments promoting our district of 24,000 students.
- Article published in *OAESA Magazine*
- Written and funded numerous grants such as Toledo Community Foundation, Lowe's etc.
- Current Mentor for all new principals in Toledo Public Schools
- Presented with students for Battelle Education App Design for The Secretary of State
- Nominated to top 20 people under 40 in Toledo

Upcoming Project

Currently in process is my second book, co-authored with Abbey Mezinko on Mastery-Based Education. This model was used with all students in Abbey's classroom with great success as all students passed the statewide math test and score *accelerated* or *advanced*. This includes students with disabilities. Be on the lookout for our publication in the forthcoming months. We have presented together at various conferences and keynotes. If interested in more information, please contact   jhunterventuregroup.com

Works Cited

Abrashoff, D. Michael. *It's Your Ship: Management Techniques from the Best Damn Ship in the Navy.* Warner Books, 2002.

Alter, Cara Hale. *The Credibility Code: How to Project Confidence & Competence When It Matters Most.* Meritus Books, 2012.

Bilas, Jay. *Toughness: Developing True Strength on and off the Court.* New American Library, 2014.

Buffum, Austin G., and Mike Mattos. *It's about Time: Planning Interventions and Extensions in Elementary School.* Solution Tree Press, 2015.

Burgess, Dave. *Teach like a Pirate.* Pirate Books

Clark, Ron. *Move Your Bus: an Extraordinary New Approach to Accelerating Success in a Work and Life.* Touchstone, 2015.

Dweck, Carol S. *Carol Dweck's Mindset: The New Psychology of Success: Summary.* Ant Hive Media, 2016.

Fullan, Michael. *Leading in a Culture of Change.* Jossey-Bass, 2014.

Jackson, Robyn Renee. *Never Underestimate Your Teachers: Instructional Leadership for Excellence in Every Classroom.* ASCD, 2013.

Kafele, Baruti K. *Principal 50: Critical Leadership Questions for Inspiring Schoolwide Excellence*, 2015

Marzano, Robert J., et al. *School Leadership That Works: From Research to Results.* Hawker Brownlow Education, 2006.

Maxwell, John C. *How Successful People Think: Change Your Thinking, Change Your Life.* Grand Central Publishing, 2009.

Maxwell, John C. *Good Leaders Ask Great Questions: Your Foundation for Successful Leadership.* Center Street, 2016.

Muhammad, Anthony. *Transforming School Culture: How to Overcome Staff Division.* Solution Tree Press, 2009.

Pattou, Edith, and Tricia Tusa. *Mrs. Spitzer's Garden.* Scholastic Inc., 2013.

Pink, Daniel H. Drive: *The Surprising Truth about What Motivates Us.* Chungrim, 2011.

Sinek, Simon. *Start with Why How Great Leaders Inspire Everyone to Take Action.* Portfolio Penguin, 2011.

Whitaker, Todd. *What Great Principals Do Differently* (2nd Edition). Eye On Education, 2011.

Whitaker, Todd. *What Great Teachers Do Differently: Seventeen Things That Matter Most.* Routledge Taylor & Francis Group, 2015.

Willis, Judy. *Learning to Love Math: Teaching Strategies That Change Student Attitudes and Get Results.* ASCD, 2010.

Wilson, Donna, and Marcus Conyers. *Teaching Students to Drive Their Brains: Metacognitive Strategies, Activities, and Lesson Ideas.* ASCD, 2016.

www.ingramcontent.com/pod-product-compliance
Lightning Source LLC
Chambersburg PA
CBHW072044290426
44110CB00014B/1567